To Liza,

Thank you for Purchasing

Know That All Things Are Possible!

Just Keep Showing Your Best

Love,
Debbie
Homeless Survivor

PARENTING

ON

PURPOSE

MENU FOR RAISING CHILDREN
IN TODAY'S SOCIETY

BY DEBORAH L. TILLMAN M.S. ED

Parenting on Purpose
by Deborah Tillman

Published 2014 by The Light Network
Copyright © Deborah L. Tillman

Printed in the United States

Interior layout by Christi Koehl

Edited by Keidi Keating

ISBN: 978-0-9571596-9-3

God shall supply all of your needs according to His riches in Glory.
~Philippians 4:19

ACKNOWLEDGMENTS

Thanks to my Lord and Savior Jesus Christ for equipping me with what I needed to do; His work here on Earth. To my loving husband, James, who has been my best friend and supporter, and to our son Zeplyn who was the catalyst for this entire journey. To my mother, Lila Washington for showing me what hard work and perseverance looks like, and to my father, James Washington, for giving me the self-confidence to reach beyond my limits. Thanks to my publicist, Cheryl Kagan, and my attorney, Ivy Bierman who have believed in me from the beginning. And to my publisher, Keidi Keating for her guidance and patience. Finally, thanks to all of the parents, families, and children who have trusted me with their hearts and have allowed me to make a difference in their lives.

This book is dedicated to those who are committed to raising their children in EXCELLENCE.

TABLE OF CONTENTS

I have fed you with milk, and not with meat: for hitherto ye were not able to bear it, neither yet now are ye able.
~I Corinthians 3:2 But...It must be told

"There can be no keener revelation of a society's soul than the way in which it treats its children."
~Nelson Mandela

FOREWORD

Everybody has a story. In 1992, my husband and I had seven horrific childcare experiences within three months concerning our son before I decided to quit my accounting job and start my own school. The first day I dropped off my son at a childcare provider's home at 8:00am. I checked on him two hours later only to find him still sitting in his car seat sweating profusely with his coat on. The final straw was when I arrived at the seventh providers home. My son was found in a back room, with the wall holding up an empty bottle that he was sucking. I quit my job the next day. I remember saying out loud over and over again, "Why is this happening to me?" I received no answer…until my question changed to, "What do you want me to do about it?" That's when I heard a still, small, but clear voice say, "I want you to do it better." At that moment, I knew my purpose, and I was introduced to the personal mission that I was to carry out here on Earth.

My heart broke for my child so much that I was willing to lose everything: my job, my income, my livelihood, my life as I knew it, in order to gain the peace, joy, and wisdom of giving a menu to this world for raising children in today's society. Although extremely painful, I realized that none of my experiences have been about me. They have been about sharing with other mothers, fathers, grandparents, Godparents, teachers, children, and anyone else who is open enough to listen. I train and teach people that they are not alone, and give them hope for their children and families if they are willing to do the work.

After twenty-one years since our son's horrific childcare experiences, my heart still bleeds, not because of my son, but because of the millions of children I did not birth. Every forty-seven seconds that ticks by a child is abused or neglected. My heart bleeds because parents are more interested in being a friend to their child than being a parent. My heart bleeds because this country has decided that the way to leave no child behind is to construct more prisons and close more schools. So I am writing this book to help parents become the best that they can be so that together our children have the opportunity to be the best they can be.

A Prayer for Our Children:

I pray for young children who are not able to speak for themselves. Bless them Lord. They did not ask to be brought into this dying world; a world where wrong is deemed right, where bad is deemed good; a world where they are neglected rather than nurtured; a world where they are abused rather than attended to; a world where children are not safe at home, in stores in schools or walking down the street. Place a hedge of protection around our children and let no hurt, harm, or danger come to them.

I pray for teenagers today who have lost their way; teenagers who are angry and carry guns and knives instead of books and Bibles. I pray for a spirit of self-control, patience, and temperance. Let them know the Truth that, "Greater is He that is in them than he that is in this world." *(1 John 4:4)*

I pray that parents today understand that being a mother or father is not about making a baby, but raising a baby. Entreat us to train our children in the way that they should go so that when they grow old they don't depart from God. Give us Godly wisdom and a better understanding. Help us to set high but reachable standards for our children and implore us to lead by example so that our children don't have to go outside of the home looking for love or a role model because they have us to look at each day.

Forgive us for every time we were impatient with our children. For when we did not spend enough time with them. For every time we didn't listen to them, learn from them, or love them unconditionally. Even when we have done all we can do please help us to trust YOU through the process, and understand that just as Hannah offered Samuel, we too must put our children in Your hands. I pray for a spirit of excellence and rebuke the spirit of mediocrity. I pray for a spirit of humility and rebuke the spirit of pride and arrogance. I pray for a spirit of obedience and rebuke the spirit of disrespect. I pray for direction. Help us trust in the Lord with all our heart and lean not to our own understanding to acknowledge You so that You may direct our paths. *(Proverbs 3:5-6)*

We thank you right now for what you are doing in our lives and in the lives of our children and families that are here with us, and those who are yet to be born. We thank you for what you are about to do, knowing that our best days are still in front of us.

Our children will be what God has called them to be because all things are possible with Christ who strengthens us. *(Philippians 4:13)*

AMEN

INTRODUCTION

WHO'S HUNGRY?

We as parents are failing our children, and I am on a mission to change that. It has taken me over seven years to write this book. So many people have asked me why it has taken such a long time to write a parenting book after working with children and families for over twenty-one years. My response is always the same. Historically the number seven has had a great significance in my life. God laid the foundation of its meaning when He introduced this number in the context of His finished Work of Creation. *(Genesis 2:2)* God introduced the Number Seven as a symbol of the completion. I have come full circle with what God has given me to give to His people. Every line in this book is inspired by the events and experiences that have happened in my life. I needed to go through the valley so that you would have victory in parenting. I needed to climb the mountains so that you would stand before a miracle. I needed to go through the trials so that you could hear about the testimony.

Through adversity there has been advancement, and through the pain I found my purpose, which is to help families come together, get it together, and stay together.

This book is designed to read like a menu. Over the past twenty-one years of operating my childcare centers and working with families, I have determined that parents are hungry and thirsty for knowledge that will provide them with the tools and techniques to raise their children in excellence.

WHY WOULD ANYONE NEED A PARENTING BOOK?

I am glad you asked. You would never think of driving anywhere without directions to where you were going; aimlessly wishing and hoping to make it to your destination without the help of your GPS. Well the same is true with parenting. You are now blessed with this precious "little one" and you have no idea how to navigate today, much less the next twenty-one plus years of their lives when the law recognizes them as adults.

As a parent, I will tell you that your role will never end until you are six feet under. And prayerfully, if you do it right, the memories, experiences and seeds of wisdom that you deposit in your child will last throughout your lifetime, and for many generations after.

That is the legacy you want to leave to your child and their children's children. If this legacy is going to happen, we as parents must rise up and begin to take back our children and families. My Greater Parenting System (GPS) will provide you with tools, techniques, and tips on how to effectively lead, guide, direct, and train your children in a way where they are able to reach their fullest potential. Just like that still, small voice I heard many years ago that said, "I want you to do it better," my assignment is to make sure that I empower you to do it better! So let's go...

My heart bleeds for what I am witnessing in homes today. In many homes, children are running circles around parents leaving them with little hope of getting through the day or having a healthy future with their children. I have witnessed first-hand children who are disrespectful, who have been given more "things" but have less appreciation for what they have been given. If one looks at the children in today's society you have to wonder what has gone wrong?

THE PROBLEM

The problem is in how children are being raised. There are two things I know for sure:

- No child that I have ever met has asked to come into this world, and...

- Although all children are born sinful *(Psalm 51:5)*, no child comes into this world as an infant operating in disrespect, disobedience and defiant behavior. The rolling of the eyes and sucking teeth are learned behaviors. This book will provide you with a candid picture of the problems, but it will also give you common sense solutions as you learn what it takes to raise children in excellence. If you are looking for a quick fix, this is not the book for you. However, if you are looking to gain insight about how to effectively raise children in a way that is pleasing to God, keep reading...

FOUR BIG PROBLEMS WITH HOW CHILDREN ARE RAISED

1. NO TIME FOR CHILDREN

I get it; we are all busy with the hustle and bustle of life. However, when you made the choice to become a parent, your meaning of time should have changed. Love to a child is spelled T.I.M.E. In the mind of a child, they think, "If you love me, you will spend time with me." Think of how many children grow up feeling that they were not loved because their parents were too busy doing something other than spending time with them. It leaves a hole in their hearts; a void that cannot be filled by eating it away, drinking it away, sexing it away, or faking it away. It won't be filled until the child realizes that regardless of their parents, God created them with His purpose in mind.

Parents are not looking into the eyes of children to see their souls anymore. They barely communicate with them. It seems like everyone is "busy" and inundated with work, activities, and things other than raising children. Riding with your child in the car to a baseball game is not what I mean by "spending time" with them. Parents are not taking time to listen to and understand children. Therefore, it becomes difficult to teach and train them. One way to change that is by eating dinner together. At the dinner table parents can communicate, bond, and strengthen relationships with their children. Even if you only have four hours at night to spend with your children give them your undivided attention instead of allowing phone calls and unfinished business to occupy your time.

2. No Communication with Children

Parents and children do not carry on conversations or even look at each other. I love to eat out and it is amazing how you can go to a restaurant and see an entire family sitting at the table physically, but not communicating at all.

Our words have been replaced by texting and emailing, instead of sitting around bonding, connecting, and talking. Communication with a child is one of the most important elements in the successful process of child development. A new generation of children should not be left to repeat all of the mistakes that have been made by us. If we take the time to communicate with them, listen to them, and really get to know our children, we can escape some of the pitfalls of the preteen years. Meaning, we won't have to guess if there is a problem, we will know them well enough to detect that there is a problem, and that it needs to be addressed. Dialogue must begin early and be continually encouraged. Don't leave this to their siblings to figure out to come and tell you. Make sure you keep the lines of communication open at all times. Raising children is about relationships, and when we don't communicate with our children we lose our children and the relationship.

3. No Limits on Technology

Technology in and of itself is not harmful. I am proud that we have made great strides in the advancement of technology. However, it is a very dangerous force that is doing much harm in America today when children have no limits or boundaries. When children get more pleasure from texting then talking, or when we put our children in front of the TV or iPad for hours a day to babysit them, and then get mad at the babysitter (TV) for not doing a good job, this is a problem. Children spend an average of 55 hours a week watching television, playing on their parents' phone or on the computer. I cannot be clearer: turn off technology and tune into your children.

In addition, violent video games also effect children, especially young children who mimic and act out what they see because they are very impressionable. Instead of removing them, or better yet not buying them, we are buried in them and wonder why our children have become bullies at school.

4. NOT LEADING BY EXAMPLE

We, as parents, emasculate our husbands, curse at our wives, and argue in front of our children saying things we ought not to. We are dishonest and then tell children not to be. We talk about our neighbors and then invite them over for a cookout. We are negative, hypocritical, and fall short of God's standard by yelling, and carrying out humiliating discipline techniques, knowing all the while that our "little ones" are watching our every move. Finally, when all heck breaks loose, we wonder how did it happen, and ask the question, "Is there any hope for us as parents?" I am here to tell you that there is hope, wisdom, guidance, and direction, and the Greater Parenting System (GPS) will take you there.

Now that we know what the problems are, let's get to the solutions.

We as parents have the responsibility to raise children of character, confidence, and conviction. Can we do it? I believe we can. Do you?

REVIEW QUESTIONS

What are the four major problems affecting children in today's society?

1. _____

2. _____

3. _____

4. _____

CHAPTER ONE

IT NOT ONLY TAKES A "VILLAGE..."
IT TAKES A PARENT.

The definition of a Parent is someone who is Positioned to Adequately Raise, Educate, Nurture and Train.

Parenting is not a right, it's a responsibility—an assignment if you will. Most of all, it is a blessing to have the privilege and opportunity to raise a human being. Part of our assignment is not to be perfect but to be the best that we can be for our children.

Each of us comes from different walks of life and various professions. We may not be the same color, nationality, or sex, nor do we all have the same number of children. But there is one thing most of us have in common: we all want the best for our children. Despite popular belief, there is a menu for getting us there.

Best is defined as that which is the most excellent. In turn, excellence has been defined in many ways, but my favorite is that offered by Ronnie Oldham, a Sales Executive and Management Professional: "Excellence is the result of *caring* more than others think is wise, *risking* more than others think is safe, *dreaming* more than others think is practical, and *expecting* more than others think is possible."

This menu is designed to help parents raise their children in excellence. That menu or series of meals does not come from me; it is uniquely designed by God to provide you with inspiration, direction, and most important, hope. That is where I want us to begin our journey through my Greater Parenting System.

Appetizer is another word for starter, and every good menu has one. When we think about raising children in excellence, we have to start with ourselves. Take a mirror, look into it, what do you see? In more cases than not, what you see is the image you are presenting to your child.

I remember working with a lady named Julie. She had just gone through a divorce and was left raising five children alone. Her ex-husband wanted nothing to do with the children. Julie had never been the disciplinarian during their eleven year marriage. She left that job to her husband. She was broken and in despair, and believed that because she had never disciplined her children, she would never be able to. So she stuck with the role she was used to: coddling, nurturing, making excuses, and telling her kids everything would be okay, when in fact it was not going to be okay until she looked in the mirror and recognized that her children saw the same image that she saw herself: DEFEAT, DESPAIR AND DISAPPOINTMENT. They responded to those images with anger, resentment, and disobedience.

After having many heart-to-heart talks with Julie she began to open up and talk about her past. She admitted that growing up her father was very domineering, and that she was often told to "sit down and shut up." As a result, she did not believe she was capable of disciplining her kids effectively, and did not want to repeat the mistakes made by her father, so she did nothing.

The first step after looking in the mirror and recognizing that you don't like what you see is to take the necessary steps to change it.

The first five years of my marriage were a struggle. I thought that once I walked down the aisle marital bliss would be the order of each day. When it was not, I thought, "I have been tricked." No one tells you during the engagement that marriage takes hard work if you are going to avoid divorce. During those first stressful years I kept asking God to change my husband.

I am going to save you the five years I wasted asking for that prayer to be answered. God is not going to change the other person until He changes things in you. No human being should have so much power that you get upset because they have a poor attitude. You cannot allow other people's mood swings, insecurities, and negativity to spill over into you. So I stopped saying, "Why are your socks all over the floor?" Instead, I just picked them up and said nothing, but by saying nothing, I was saying everything. When I would find a pair of socks in the hamper, I would say, "I appreciate the way you help me by putting your socks in the hamper. You're the best, honey."

It sounds crazy, but it is so effective. When you build people up as opposed to tearing them down, life becomes so much better for everyone. So now, twenty-two years later, I am much happier and more at peace in my marriage, not because God changed my husband but because God changed me. My actions helped to bring about the change I always hoped for in my husband. It is the same with your children. Parents and families do not get better by osmosis. They have to take action and try something different in order to get a different result. If you are looking in the mirror and see negativity, generational curses, abuse, neglect, gossiping, lying, cheating, stealing, guilt, shame, low esteem, or victimhood, those are things you are passing along to your children. We can only give our children what we have in ourselves, and if we do not first rid ourselves of the poison inside of us, our children will suffer.

SET THE STANDARD!

Centuries ago, plumblines were used. A plumbline was a cord with a lead weight used by builders to make sure that the walls were constructed straight up and down. A plumbline was also used to test existing walls to see whether they had settled and tilted, needing to be torn down.

I heard a metaphor about two men who were constructing buildings side by side. The first builder built his foundation and walls without checking it with a plumbline, to see if it was level. He looked at the foundation and walls and said, "It looks level, so that's good enough for me." The second builder built his foundation and walls, carefully using a plumbline after each level of stones were added.

When both builders were finished building their buildings, a building inspector came. He said to the first builder, "It looks good from the outside but let's check it to see if it is level and straight." Finding that the foundation and walls were crooked, he said to the builder, "the foundations and walls are crooked. If a storm comes then your building will fall down. Your building must be torn down, and then you must start over and build it right." The inspector then went over to the second builder and checked his foundation and walls. Satisfied, he told the second builder, "It couldn't have been any better than if I had built it myself. Go ahead and use the building."

The moral of the story is that in order to build a solid foundation for our children we have to set the standard; a plumbline if you will. If we, as parents, are not ourselves plumb and level, it is going to be difficult to give our children the tools they need to excel. I know you are thinking that is easier said than done. How can we do that?

STEP I

First, write the Vision for yourself and your children. The Bible scripture Habakkuk 2:2 says: "Write the vision, and make it plain on tablets, that he may run that readeth it."

You must have a Vision for what you want for your child. I don't mean an occupation, such as a doctor, a lawyer or an engineer, I am talking about character traits, such as honesty, trustworthiness, compassion, hard working, and respectful. Once you have the Vision written then the second step is to begin working as a parent within the outline of that Vision. "Our assignment as parents is to train children in the way they should go, so even when they grow old, they will not depart from it." *(Proverbs 22:6 KJV)*

SAMPLE VISION STATEMENT (FOR CHILD)
The vision for our son, Zeplyn Tillman, is that he will grow up in the admonition of the Lord. It is our vision that Zeplyn will be honest, trustworthy, and compassionate, always seeking wisdom, knowledge and understanding in the choices he makes. And that he will use his gifts, talents, and abilities to help others in this world always being mindful and having the faith to know that God is in control and has the best plan for his life. We trust that God will order his steps so that he reaches his divine destiny.

SAMPLE VISION STATEMENT (FOR PARENT)
To religiously educate, nurture, lead, guide, and direct my child by providing him with the best example physically, spiritually, and emotionally. To train him in the way he should go and to discipline in love not in fear or anger. To selflessly protect and provide for the needs of my child according to God's riches in glory, and to teach my child about love, faith, goodness, and compassion. To learn from my child by listening, communicating, and bonding with him. To be prayerful and patient in every decision that I make concerning the welfare of my child, and to be obedient to what the Spirit says.

God has placed all of us in charge of training our children. Imagine that? If you and I are going to train, we need to be in shape physically, spiritually, and emotionally to get through the journey successfully. Taking care of ourselves is one of the most important things we can do when raising children. What does it matter if we do all of these wonderful things in the book, and if we apply all of the tools and techniques yet do not live long enough or healthy enough to see it through?

I Corinthians 6:19 says that our bodies are the temple of the Holy Ghost. What that means is that God dwells inside of you and me. So whatever our task as parents from the time our children are born until we die, the God inside of you and I is strong enough to raise happy, healthy, productive human beings if we set the standard, work hard, and believe it.

If we are too tired to run after our children when they take off, or we are too impatient because we have just filled our stomachs with junk food and sweets, we are not going to be any good physically or emotionally for this journey called parenting. Stop and make the decision to CHANGE NOW.

STEP II - LEAD BY EXAMPLE

The old saying, the apple doesn't fall far from the tree is an understatement. Children learn to act, behave, speak, and react to situations by watching their parents. If Mom is constantly yelling, being negative, and disrespecting others, most likely her children will do the same. If Dad sits around all day expecting someone to wait on him, and can't even take out the trash, his sons will likely grow up doing the same thing and wishing for a maid. Do as I say, not as I do doesn't work for this generation of children. What they see you do they will want to do because you are their role models whether you like it or not. As parents, we must know that we are the leaders of the family not the children. There have been so many instances when I have heard parents asking the child, "Are you ready for dinner?" "What do you want to eat?" "Do you want to go to church?" "Are you ready to get up and go to school?" Really? I know it sounds harsh but until the child is responsible enough to put the food on the table, put clothes on their backs, and pay for the roof over their heads, we the parents need to be in control of those decisions. They don't get to negotiate that.

Give your child someone to look up to by stating it is time to eat, be ready at 8am for school, and we are all going to church. The emphasis is on "all." Stop sending your child to church without you. What message does that send? If you are going to church, then the entire household needs to go. Parents like to say, "My child won't do this or that." You are the parent, they are the children, and as long as they are living under your roof they don't have a choice in certain matters. That is how you teach obedience at an early age.

Parents also have a very interesting way of "telling" their children not to smoke, drink, or use profanity to name a few, yet they smoke, drink, and use profanity. It is hypocritical and does not make much sense to tell a child to do something that you the parent are not willing to do. It sends mixed signals and children don't have a problem throwing it right back in your face. Children should have a reason other than the fact that you birthed them to look up to you. That is our assigned position as parents.

I don't care where you are right now, what struggle or adversity you are suffering from, or how many mistakes you have made, you can make the choice right now to change your mindset. Believe in yourself, rise up, and become the parent God has designed for you to be.

Greatness only happens when you attempt to walk in it.

Feast on Wisdom Food

Your beliefs become your thoughts
Your thoughts become your words
Your words become your actions
Your actions become your habits
Your habits become your values
Your values become your destiny.

~Mahatma Gandhi

CHAPTER TWO

We become who we are by the choices we make. So choose to parent in excellence.

After eating the appetizer, we are ready to make choices about which entre we will decide upon. The next eight choices I am going to present to you will be things that you can choose to do or not to do. If you choose not to do them, trust and know that there will be consequences that will show up in the areas of your child's Attitude, Behaviors, Confidence, and eventually their Destiny (A,B,C,D's).

THE FIRST CHOICE IS TO EXPECT THE BEST FROM CHILDREN.

Feast on this wonderful quote from Karen Rayn:

> *Only as high as I reach can I grow*
> *Only as far as I seek can I go*
> *Only as deep as I look can I see*
> *Only as much as I dream can I be.*

God has a plan and a purpose for your child: Jeremiah

29:11 says, "I know the plans I have for you and they are of good not evil to take you to your expected end." That is the promise of God.

God has the plan for your child, but we as parents must do everything in our power to see that our children have the best opportunity to reach their Divine Destiny.

Your motto should be: "The sky is the limit. Reach for the moon and even if you miss you will be amongst the stars." Repeating this over and over to your child will let them know that you, the most important person in their lives (for now), believes in them. I can't tell you how many parents have killed the dreams of their children. Since they are doubters and because they have not accomplished much in their lives—most likely because someone told them they would never be able to accomplish anything—they tell their children what they cannot be. It becomes the generational "lie" that gets carried down from generation to generation. Break the chain and give your child something you didn't have growing up: HOPE and CONFIDENCE.

Expecting the best means that you are also aiming high for your children.

Aiming high does two things:

- Moves children forward
- Gives children encouragement

Children with parents who have high expectations for them tend to strive to reach them because they know their parents believe in them. They begin to think, "If I can get a grade 'B' why not strive for an 'A?'"

My parents never allowed 'C' grades to come into the house. To them it meant average and their three girls were not average. So their expectations became my expectations. I figured if they think that I can do better and am not an average student, then let me work my hardest so that they know their expectations of me are correct. At ten-years-old, I am sure my reasoning was not that sound, all I knew was that my parents believed in me so I better believe in myself.

I am currently working with two parents whose child is not doing well in the 9th grade. He is actually doing horrible. He is getting D's and F's on his report card. He is withdrawn and only wants to hang out with so-called friends. The problem I had with these parents is when the father commented, "Well I know his grades are bad but he is not on drugs and he has not gotten any girl pregnant and he is not as bad as (Jerry's) child so it could be worse." Yes, it could be worse but it also could be a whole lot better. Are we aiming so low that we have gotten to the point where we are comparing our sons and daughters to other people's children?

The fact of the matter is that it hurts to see any child failing but let's not cover a wound with a band-aid, as it won't heal. Let's fix the problem. The grades are bad due to poor study habits, not doing the work, and needing a tutor. There are reasons. Find out what the reason is and then do the work to fix the problem. Comparing my wound to your wound won't heal the wound.

Also, aiming high gives children encouragement. One of my favorite children's books is *The Little Engine that Could* by Watty Piper. This is a great book used to teach the values of hard work and perseverance. I love the lines from the book, "I think I can I think I can." It reinforces that if you inevitably think you can then you will begin to act on what you think you can do.

Let me give you an example. Many parents of young children that I work with around the country don't have high expectations of their children. I own childcare centers that begin with children attending at the age of three months, and I can tell you without a doubt that high expectations play a major role in children gaining confidence and responsibility early on.

For example, your toddler should:

- Understand that falling out in a tantrum is not going to get them anything
- Talking back and hitting you is not okay
- Misbehaving will have a consequence
- Come to you when you call them
- Listen to you when you speak
- Remain seated at the dinner table.

When we as parents don't expect much from our children or contend that they don't understand because they are too young, we are underestimating them. In essence, we are stifling them because we are not allowing them to do the things they are very capable of doing if we took the time to teach them. A child who falls out in the store when he or she has been told "no" to having candy will continue to fall out based on the response from the parent. If we are too embarrassed to correct the behavior and "give in" by letting them have the candy, that is not the child being disobedient, that is us, the parents, not fulfilling our assignment, which is to "TRAIN" the child in the way they "SHOULD" go, not how they WANT to go.

THE SECOND CHOICE IS TO *ELIMINATE THE GUILT.*

We, as parents, feel guilty about spending 10 to 14 hours away from our children. We feel guilty about the spouses we have chosen, especially if they have not lived up to our expectations. We feel guilty about not being able to provide our children with all of the "best" in our minds that we think they deserve. We feel guilty about not being able to provide children with the "newest" most expensive gadget. We just plain feel guilty about everything: the houses we live in, the circumstances we are in, the fact that we have all made some poor choices in our lives that have led to dire consequences, and so on.

We all have things we could choose to feel rightfully guilty about—things we could have done better but did not, or times we blew it and did something against our values or family rules. There are 86,400 seconds in a day, and if the enemy had his way, he would use every one of them attempting to help us feel guilty. I worked with a woman named Margaret who felt guilty about everything. Guilty about having to work long hours, guilty about spending so much time away from her son due to the commute, guilty about the mate she had chosen who never bothered to see their son. Guilt will eat you up so much that you will not be able to see the blessings that you do have. One of my favorite scriptures is Romans 8:28. Read it and allow it to get into your spirit. All things really do work together for the good of those who love the Lord and are called according to His purpose. If your son's dad or mother is no longer around, and you are walking with God, thank Him. If you have a job that takes you away from your family, but you are able to afford excellent childcare or a nanny to help out, thank Him. In the end, the good, bad, and ugly all work together.

Guilt is a toxin that will keep you from moving forward and living in a state of peace and joy. You and I cannot do anything about our past, and it makes no sense to keep rehearsing it over and over again. You can never drive forward if you keep looking in your rear view mirror. Focus on the here and now. We can only learn from the past and not make the same mistakes twice so that our present and futures are better and brighter.

Living in the "would haves," "could haves," and "should haves" state will only make you frustrated. Guilt can debilitate you if you allow it to. It is time to get rid of the guilt, learn from the mistakes of the past, and try to do the very best you can for your children in the future.

*THE THIRD CHOICE IS TO **ERASE FEAR.***

Fear was the first human emotion recorded in Genesis 3:10, and do not fear is mentioned 366 times in the Bible. We have a fear of failing, a fear of succeeding, a fear of being a parent, a fear of what we are going to have to "give up" in order to raise our children in excellence, fear of being embarrassed about what other people say about the way we raise our children, and so on. We are laced in fear and depending on whether the fear factor is stronger than our ability to make the choice to let it go, some men and women walk away from the entire journey becoming absentee moms and dads.

But God does not give us a spirit of fear. He gives us power, love, and a sound mind to press through the fear. *(2 Timothy 1:7)*

I have learned over the years that fear will paralyze you. I ran into a high school classmate ten years ago. She talked about having two wonderful children and how she was in the process of writing a book about the process it took to raise two boys as a single mother. We spoke for a while. I encouraged her, and she went on her way. Several years later, I ran into her again. She brought up the fact that she never wrote that book. I asked her why? And she told me that she was afraid of what other people would say if she put pen to paper. I could not believe what I heard. My high school classmate had gone through 35 years of her life and she was still feeling the weight of what other people would say about her. One thing I know for sure is that people have no heaven or hell to put you in. Didn't she realize that her writing the book was never about her? It was about helping some other single mom who could have been blessed through her experiences.

THE FOURTH CHOICE IS TO **EVALUATE YOUR WORDS.**

Words are so powerful and are designed to either build up or tear down. The power of words spoken by a parent can either make or break a child. Words are life changing and long lasting.

Use your words to encourage, inspire, and motivate your child, not discourage and dishearten them. Have you ever noticed how someone can give you ten compliments and make one discouraging comment, and you will only remember the negative? Some adults are still suffering from the words a parent spoke into their lives when they were very young, but they have never forgotten.

Change Your Words
Parents have heard me say there are four words we should try to avoid when talking to children. They are 'naughty,' 'bad,' 'good,' and 'no.' Instead of saying 'good boy/girl,' try using 'clever.' 'That's clever! I like the way you did this or that.' It is more descriptive when you use those words. Try to turn a negative comment into a positive one. For example, 'stop whining' could be replaced with, 'please ask me with your friendly voice.' Instead of saying "no," explain to the child what to do. Children love to please, and they respond positively to encouragement and praise.

Positive words bring us confidence and negative words can cripple us with inferiority. My mother used to say, "If you can't say anything nice, don't say anything at all." Every time you open your mouth, try to speak words of life not death. Children should never hear you say, "You are just like your father or mother" in a negative context. They should not hear you say, "You will never amount to anything."

I know that life has us all feeling frustrated and stressed out at times, but when you are raising a child your assignment is too great, too enormous, too impacting not to take a moment and calm down. Walk away for a minute and breathe rather than saying something you will regret later. If you do say something that you regret, be the example by going to your child and apologizing. An "I am sorry for not calming myself before I spoke to you in that manner" will go much farther than not apologizing and allowing resentment and anger to brew.

Watch Your Tone of Voice
Yelling at children creates tension in the air and bad vibes in the house. In order for your house to become a home that will be a safe haven for your family, you have to keep the tone down and use your inside voice.

Transform Criticism into Compliments
Have you ever stopped to listen to yourself? I hear parents criticizing everything their child does. They sound like a broken record shouting commands like: "stop, no, don't, listen" over and over. Yet when the child is playing nicely they never say anything. Children and some adults love attention. For a child, attention gives them energy. If you call my name I love that attention whether it is in a negative way or a positive way. Why not focus your attention on the positive that you can provide for your child rather than the negative? If you criticize children often, they feel like failures. When you inspire through encouragement and compliments, they don't give up as easily and become more successful. Use uplifting phrases such as "Keep at it; you're almost there," "I'm impressed with your effort," and "You're getting the hang of it now."

Use Love Names
Avoid name calling. Your child is not lazy, clumsy, bratty, spoiled (only if you made them that way) stupid, silly or an idiot. Instead change your words to fabulous, awesome, tell them "there is greatness in you" or "you are too smart to have misbehaved." I know your mother or father may have said those words to you growing up, but this is your child and they deserve better.

Catch Children Doing Something Right
Look for the good qualities in your child and describe what you see. When you see your child being kind, trying hard, being brave, helping another child, reading a book, making their bed, tell them how impressed you are.

Remember that life and death is in the power of the tongue. Blessings and curses don't come out of the same mouth. I cannot tell you how important your words are when you are raising children. When they are young, they hang onto your every word. As they get older, your words become more and more powerful, and if said often enough, children believe it. Speak those things that are not as though they were until they are.

THE FIFTH CHOICE IS TO *ELEVATE YOUR THINKING ON DISCIPLINE.*

Discipline comes from the Latin word "disciplinare" which means to TEACH. Presently, it is often only associated with punishment but actually means much more than that. Effective discipline occurs in a positive, supportive, loving parent-child relationship; uses positive reinforcement to promote desired behaviors (proactive) and uses punishment (when necessary) to decrease or eliminate undesired or ineffective behaviors.

When we elevate our thinking on discipline it means not to take one verse from the Old Testament to justify why the first reaction to your child's negative behavior is spanking him or her. In many homes including my own, I grew up hearing "spare the rod, spoil the child" which comes from Proverbs 13:24 in the bible, "He who spares the rod hates his son, but he who loves him is careful to discipline him." The operative word is "careful." What I am witnessing in American homes are people who are being "careless" in disciplining their children and therefore, children are suffering from a hidden epidemic of child abuse and neglect.

The Bible verses that are most commonly used by some to teach that Christian parents should spank their children come entirely from the Old Testament and are as follows:

Proverbs 22:15 "Foolishness is bound in the heart of a child; but the rod of correction shall drive it far from him."

Proverbs 23:13-14 "Withhold not correction from the child: for if you beat him with the rod, he shall not die. Thou shalt beat him with the rod, and shall deliver his soul from hell."

Proverbs 29:15 "The rod and reproof give wisdom: but a child left to himself brings his mother to shame."

According to Charles F. Creech, author of *Should Christian Parents spank their Children?* (2003), there is an important question to ask about these verses from the Old Testament. Do they apply today in the same way that they did during the times of the Old Testament, or are these verses other examples of the harshness of the "law" that are no longer to be applied in the way they once were because we live in the age of grace? The bible does not change so the same principle still applies, in that children still need to have the proper amount of correction, but the correction should not be applied with corporal punishment. If we are going to take some of the verses of the Old Testament that have to do with the punishment of children and apply them all literally, then we should take all of the verses in the Old Testament that have to do with the punishment of children and apply them all literally. For example, in Deuteronomy 21:18-21 it says, "If a man has a stubborn and rebellious son, which will not obey the voice of his father, or the voice of his mother, and that, when they have chastened him, will not hearken unto them: Then shall his father and his mother lay hold on him and bring him out unto the elders of his city, and unto the gate of his place; and they shall say unto the elders of his city, This our son is stubborn and rebellious, he will not obey our voice; he is a glutton and a drunkard. And all the men of his city shall stone him with stones, that he die: so shalt thou put evil away from among you; and all Israel shall hear and fear." Of course, no one teaches that we should apply this passage in Deuteronomy to our current day or that we should apply it when we correct our children today. Why? Because we recognize that the passage in Deuteronomy was for a different age and a different time. It is much too harsh for the day in which we live. We can look at the verses in Proverbs that have to do with using a "rod" on a child in the same way even if we interpret these parts of Proverbs literally. A good and valid interpretation of the Bible is to say that the above verses from Deuteronomy and the Proverbs are among the things from the Old Testament that are a part of the harshness and strictness of the law that should not be applied in our day because of the difference between the Old Testament and the New Testament and because of the difference between the law and the grace and truth which came by Jesus Christ. *(John 1:17)*.

If we give a symbolic meaning to the verses in Proverbs, then the "rod of correction" would simply mean that correction is a rod. Compare Proverbs 14:3 where the word "rod" is used in another context that does not involve the correction of children, and very obviously does not involve a literal rod either. It says, "In the mouth of the foolish is a rod of pride: but the lips of the wise shall preserve them." This verse means that pride is a rod. It does not mean that there is a literal rod or stick in the mouth of a foolish person. We do not have to interpret the phrase "rod of correction" as a literal rod either.

Further in the book of First Corinthians Paul was writing to the believers in the city of Corinth, and one of the reasons that he was writing was to correct problems that existed among the Christians there. Some of the believers in Corinth were involved in things that they ought not to be involved with. Paul wrote to them and said in First Corinthians 4:21, "What will you? shall I come unto you with a rod, or in love, and in the spirit of meekness? Paul was not saying that he might come with a literal rod and strike them. He was talking about his attitude when he came to correct them in person. He was asking them if they preferred him to be stern or to be compassionate? As Proverbs 14:3 shows and as First Corinthians 4:21 shows, when a Bible verse contains the word "rod" in regards to the correction of someone, no one is obligated to interpret it as referring to a literal rod. It is consistent with other parts of scripture to say that a rod is often symbolic when used in reference to correcting someone.

Additionally, I often hear parents say they beat their children because their parents or grandparents did it and they turned out fine. The truth of the matter is that none of us are really "fine." We all have some issue, insecurity or idiosyncrasy that we need to work on. I don't think that knocking a child upside their head is teaching them any positive life lesson. Violence begets violence. The Bible instructs us not to provoke our children to anger. *(Ephesians 6:4)* It is also very clear that our responsibility as parents is to discipline in love not in anger. Spanking children as soon as they do something you don't like sets up a loop of bad behavior. God does not sanction bruises and whelps on the body of children.

Corporal punishment instills fear rather than understanding. Even if children stop the negative behavior when spanked which rarely happens, that doesn't mean they get why they shouldn't have been acting out in the first place. In addition, beatings set a bad example, teaching children that aggressive behavior is a solution to their problems and we have the nerve to question why now in 2014, the world is so violent. Could it be attributed to what we have taught our children? If you are angry to the point where you cannot control what you do or say, take a moment to calm down. Parents can lovingly administer discipline by teaching and training their child in a calm manner. Stop and think before you react and speak. You are teaching your child a life lesson when you remain calm because they see and understand that you can correct them without losing control. Parents should never discipline a child when they are uncontrollably angry. Remember, some young strong-willed children will push your buttons and it is normal to become angry with them. However, the more you practice the fruit of the spirit *(Galatians 5)* the more you will be able to gain control over your character and emotions. Try these helpful suggestions below.

Love is actively training and teaching our children—diligently. *(Deuteronomy 6:6-7)* Put consistent and loving effort into being an active parent daily.

Love is providing for your children's physical needs. *(II Corinthians 12:4)*

Discipline with consistency. *(Proverbs 29:17)*

Love involves the promotion of Biblical teaching to your children early. *(Psalm 34:11)* The best teachings are by example. Children imitate what they see more than what they are told. Therefore, model the behavior you want to see. Finally, follow God's pattern, as He disciplines us, for our own good. *(Hebrews 12:5-11)* we should lovingly discipline our children. Be steadfast in correction, yet giving encouragement and praise where it is due.

Don't mistake my quest for positive discipline with permissive parenting. I believe as the bible instructs to correct children. I also believe in giving children consequences for negative behavior. That is how they learn. We don't get angry with and correct children we don't love. Because we love our children, we must correct them in a manner that will teach them not only a lesson for a moment but also lessons for a lifetime.

THE SIXTH CHOICE IS TO **EDUCATE AND EMPOWER CHILDREN.**

Stop leaving all of the teaching to the educators, schools, or worse TV to do for your child what you should be doing for them. Parents are a child's first teacher. No human should be more invested in your child than you. I can't tell you how many children come to my preschool at 4-years-old and are not ready to go to kindergarten, not because they don't know their letters and numbers but because they have no social skills and very limited social-emotional intelligence or self-control. Despite popular opinion it is not the teacher's job to raise our children. The responsibility is in our hands as parents.

If a child tells you they don't want to do homework, your response should be, "Homework is non-negotiable, and talk to me about why you are saying you don't want to do homework. Is it too difficult? Can I help you? Do you need a tutor?"

If the child says they don't want to go to school, your response needs to be, "Not going to school is not an option." Talk about why you have to go to work and if you did not what the consequences would be. There would also be consequences to them not going to school. Discuss them, make a list of pros and cons of not going to school. After you go through all of that, trust that they will be rushing you out of the house running to school. Children don't want to take the time to think through what the results of their choices would be. It is your job to show them.

Educate by Teaching Values
There are things that cannot wait, like the training of a child in the way that he should go. Our time with our children is running out. It is slipping away, and God is still holding you and I responsible.

Educate your child to have values. It is important for children to understand the value of telling the truth.

All have lied and come short of pleasing their parents. You bring that cute bundle of joy home and just wait two years, sometimes as early as 18 months, and it begins. Johnny is crying on the floor, your beautiful child is standing over him with a toy in her hand that is not hers and you ask, "Did you take that toy from Johnny?" Your child looks at you with those endearing eyes, the toy in her hand, and very authoritatively says, "No I didn't" or my favorite "un uh."

We would all love to raise children that understand the value of being truthful. However, good morals and character traits don't just happen. Television, video games, and schools are not equipped to teach children what parents should be teaching in the home. The following are some significant tools to consider while raising your precious "little ones" to be honest:

1. *Take away the "fear factor"*

Find out the reason behind the lie, as it helps you understand your child's needs. In most cases, children lie out of fear. They are afraid of the consequences, of being exposed or simply not wanting to be embarrassed. If they know that they can be honest with you about what's on their mind without you getting mad or critical, they will come to realize that honesty is the best approach. Explain to children that if they are honest the first time you ask them, no matter how bad it is, they will not get in trouble, and then keep your promise.

2. *Praise and celebrate honesty*

Children like attention and approval can be very

appealing. Let your children know that you value and appreciate the truth. Encourage your children each and every time they tell the truth, particularly if you have reprimanded them before for lying. Praise boosts self-confidence and encourages positive behavior.

3. STOP name calling

When children lie, refrain from saying things like "you are nothing but a liar." Instead say, "I am not pleased with your behavior and I know that you are capable of doing better." As I mentioned earlier, make a habit of speaking life and destiny into your children rather than negativity and despair. Remember, as long as you are breathing, there is always hope for children to get another chance to tell the truth.

4. Don't send "mixed messages"

If you are feeling frustrated and your child asks you how you are doing? Don't say, "I am fine." They do not have to know details, but they do need to know you have had better days. When parents are dishonest about their emotions, children learn to hide behind a happy face or a response that says everything is "ok" even when it is not. That creates feelings of insecurity and low self-esteem because children are trying to be something they are not.

5. Model honesty for your children

The most important tool any parent can use is to practice what you preach. Parents should not ask their children not to lie, yet the parents lie. "Do as I say, not as I do," is not an effective way to teach children core values. Those little white lies about not being home when an annoying neighbor telephones who you do not wish to speak to, or the gift that a friend gave you that you simply detest despite the smile on your face, all add up in your child's eyes as dishonesty.

The best we can offer our children as parents is to lead, guide, and direct them toward truth. The rest will be up to them to choose honesty over dishonesty. One thing we know for sure, both have long lasting outcomes.

Truth does not have to be painful: The Four "P's" of Teaching Values

Be Patient – Some children will lie right to your face and that is when this concept has to kick in. If children see their parents taking the time to teach them in a manner that is warm and inviting, it becomes easier for the children to connect to the value.

Be Persistent – Telling the truth does not happen overnight. Some grown-ups have not yet mastered it. However, when parents begin to teach children at a young age and use every lie and truth as a "teachable moment" it is priceless.

Be Passionate – Parents must be the most invested in building core values and character traits in children.

Be Positive – Everyone makes mistakes and children are no different. Through every lie there is a lesson to be learned and that must bring us Joy!

The second point is to Empower Children

I hear children and parents say, "I can't, they can't." Take the "T" out of can't because you CAN always try. When we empower our children, they develop the skills they need to have power over their own lives.

In the short-term empowerment plants the seeds for developing an "I can do it" attitude. In the long-term, empowerment helps children become capable and accountable and develop high self-esteem in their teen and adult lives.

Teaching life skills empowers your kids and helps them develop that priceless internal dialogue "Yes, I can!"

You do that by:

- Increasing a child's self-awareness Ask them questions that make them respond. If they can talk they can respond. Stop allowing children to get by with shaking or nodding their heads in agreement.
- Stop speaking for children when they can speak for themselves.
- Stop making excuses for why your child isn't doing something.
- Stop solving problems they can solve for themselves. Offer support, and allow them to figure it out.
- Don't give them the answer. For older kids with good verbal skills, ask questions to children that encourage them to explore their own solutions to problems. Then encourage them to choose a solution and follow through. Offer support along the way. For little ones, gently coaching with suggestions sets the groundwork, "Perhaps he'll give you the toy if you offer him another one?" is one example.
- Finally, let go. I had a friend who didn't like the

:

way her child made up his bed. He was seven and often attempted to make it by balling up the flat sheet and putting the comforter on as neatly as he could. It's so much easier to jump in and do things for kids. Avoid the temptation to do this. It's not worth the time savings when a parent jumps in and solves the problem for the child. In these instances, kids are learning they can't do it, or can't do it well enough to please their parents, and therefore aren't good enough.

EXAMPLE: The bed they made might look bad, the clothes may not match, you might be ten minutes late waiting for those shoes to go on but even if they are on the wrong feet, the end result is that your child did it himself, and that's priceless.

THE SEVENTH CHOICE IS TO *ENJOY THE JOURNEY.*

1. Take time with your child. We as parents have a very small window of opportunity to do many things. From birth to ten-years-old we talk, train and teach our children the way they should go. From eleven years to twenty-years-old, we should listen, learn them all over again and love them through the many mistakes they will eventually make.

2. Treat your child with respect. They learn respect from you and the way you treat others while driving, while in the grocery store, while at school. You have many instances in which to teach your child by showing them. So don't miss valuable teachable moments.

Not everyone gets to be a parent. You have been given a

tremendous GIFT and your responsibility is to LOVE them unconditionally. It is a journey and immediate changes don't happen overnight.

"Plenty of people miss their share of happiness, not because they never found it, but because they didn't stop to enjoy it."

~William Feather

This principal has a special meaning for me and is one I think many of us forget in our busy lives. But what does it really mean? Life is a Journey not a Destination; it is about living in the present. It's not about not having goals, but it is about working so hard to reach your goals or being so focused on "getting there" that you forget to enjoy today. Tomorrow is not promised to any of us. If you are working so much that you are missing Christmas concerts, parent teacher conferences, and extracurricular activities like little league, ballet recitals, and graduations, you will need to re-evaluate your priorities. Children want to see you in the stands cheering for them, wishing them well, and believing in them. Being supportive does not mean arguing with other parents, or screaming at someone else's child because they missed the buzzer beater shot in basketball. If you are truly leading by example then you are cheering for everybody's child. Yes, there can only be one winner on the basketball court, but we can all be winners in America, when our children are raised with a solid foundation for future success.

*THE EIGHTH CHOICE IS TO **ENDURE TO THE END.***

I tell parents that walk into the doors of my school

everyday that as long as they are blessed to wake up every morning with breath in their body, they have another opportunity to do better and to be better. Parents often say, "I don't know what to do so I am giving up." My response is, "You don't get the chance to give up." When you had the baby, it became a lifelong commitment to raise the child.

I want you to know that you are not alone on this parenting journey. As long as the Lord wakes us up every morning with the activity of our limbs, we all have another opportunity to help our children be the best they can be. Remember the race not given to the swift but to the one who endures to the end. Galatians 6:9 says, Let us not be weary in well doing for in due season we will reap if we faint not.

The next part of the meal is the main course or the "entre."

CHAPTER THREE

ME(A)T AND RISE ABOVE THE CHALLENGES

"I have told you these things, so that in me you may have peace. In this world you will have trouble. But take heart! I have overcome the world." *(John 16:33)*

Parents don't get menus on how to raise children (until now). We all have ups and downs and make many mistakes along the way. Difficult times can be more readily endured if we retain the conviction that our existence holds a purpose to achieve, a cause to pursue, a child to love, and a destiny to reach.

What do Diamonds, Gold, Butterflies, and Parents have in common?

A Diamond starts as carbon, which undergoes intense heat, high pressure and a tremendous squeezing process to become brilliant.

Gold is made by a process called refining. It involves enormous levels of heat to ensure that the impurities are removed before it can be made into something desirable.

Butterflies begin as creepy, crawly caterpillars that look anything but beautiful, yet through the process of transformation they evolve over time into brilliant, colorful, amazing butterflies.

Parents must begin to realize that anything with an amazing destiny must undergo a *tremendous process*. Going through the process, as painful as it may be, is the only way for God to make and mold us and our children into what He created us to be.

Remember, "I can do all things through Christ who strengthens me."—Even being a Great Parent. *(Philippians 4:13)*

Some of the things that you are going to face on this parenting journey are outlined in this chapter. It is imperative that before every challenge, situation, circumstance or decision you must do one thing: PRAY WITHOUT CEASING. *(I Thessalonians 5:17)*

HOW TO HANDLE *ATTITUDES*

I wanted to talk about attitudes because at a certain age, usually around the preteens, you will begin to think that you did not birth your child. They become different people. They are moody, indecisive, and have 'tudes' as I call them. As parents we must understand that our children are going through peer pressure, puberty, insecurities, and although we sympathize with them, we cannot excuse their negative behavior. When your child is going through this stage, you are *not* going to want to be around them because they are so negative, introverted, and unhappy. However, this is the time to cling close to your child. You can sit in silence but don't leave them. This is not the time to lecture them with sayings like "your attitude will determine your altitude" because they won't hear you. Just let them know that when they are ready to talk, you will be there. Make it clear to them that the rules will change from using gentle touches to keeping bedroom doors open, and that there will be no retreating into their headphones in silence. As long as they are living under your roof, know that you do have control.

HOW TO HANDLE *DRUGS AND ALCOHOL*

When children are raised to believe that there is greatness in them from a young age, and expectations are high for them, the first conversation you are going to have with them about drugs and alcohol, is not when they are 18-years-old. Any substance that has the ability to affect the mind and body of your child must not be tolerated. People often ask, "How did you keep your son away from drugs in a world where they are rampant?" The answer really is by the grace of God and instilling in my son as soon as he could understand that drugs were very bad and that they would alter the vision we had for him and his destiny. We also talked seriously about the effects of drugs and alcohol use as he got older and never missed an opportunity to provide an example. We probably scared him to death!

We also had no problem going through backpacks, and personal belongings. There is "no total privacy" when your young child is living in your house under your roof.

HOW TO HANDLE **YOUR CHILD'S FRIENDS**

You must be mindful of who your child's friends are. Yes, you heard me right. Children should not be spending time with "friends" you don't know. Watch for changes in clothing, personal appearance, and hygiene. Although your child's body is his or her own, you are still the parent and thereby you need to approve certain things as parents especially before allowing teenagers to wear makeup, get piercings, and tattoos. I remember my young son attempting to go outside of the home when he was 13 with a do wrag on his head. My husband told him to not even think about going outside of the house with it on his head. Why? Not for any other reason except PERCEPTION. We live in a world where young African American men are still measured by the way they look rather than what is on the inside of them. It was evident to us very early on that we needed to explain to our young son that we know your character and loving spirit but if you "look" a certain way, others will judge you by the way you look rather than getting to know who you are. Parents often tell me that their children need to show their individuality. That is fine when they are old enough to take care of their "individuality" expenses, as then they can make the choice to look a certain way. By that time, they would have probably grown out of the phase, prayerfully.

HOW TO HANDLE **SLEEPOVERS**

Do not allow your child to spend the night at the homes of parents you do not know whose parenting styles you don't agree with, or parents that you do not have a relationship with. I am talking about the casual friend at your child's baseball game that you met. You want to know what kind of home they keep and understand that the same things that do not go on at your house should not be going on at their home either, such as smoking, drinking, having sex or experimenting with drugs, or else they will not be permitted to go. Is it being judgmental? No, it is just saying, "I am the parent and I will be deciding who is not good for you since you are not privy to having that much wisdom and discernment yet." The sleepovers happened at my house, not outside of the house or there were no sleepovers. You never want to send your child to the home of parents you have no idea about or don't know if they are home or not. Make sure to check out everything. Don't take your child's word for it especially at the preteen age. They are often afraid to ask you because they have made up in their minds that you will say no and instead of being turned down, they won't ask. You would never forgive yourself if something detrimental happened all because you did not take the time to establish a connection and relationship, which often takes years with the parents of your child's close friends.

HOW TO HANDLE **BEDTIME MAYHEM**

The key in establishing a child's bedtime routine is to delineate betwen what your child needs and what your child wants. The stakes are high. Insufficient sleep affects a child's attitude, behavior and development. Here are some helpful tips on how to create the ritual for a peaceful good night sleep.

Bedtime tips:
Spend time unwinding with a quiet activity 30 minutes before starting the bedtime routine. It will settle the body, mind and spirit. Be consistent. The routine should be the same night to night so that your child learns to anticipate sleep as part of the routine.

Include bath-time in your regular routine, as the soothing warmth will help prepare your child's body for rest. Whenever you start something like co sleeping and having children sleep with the television on, you are going to have to continue it. If you don't want to break a habit don't start a habit that you don't want to continue. Again, let me say that many people will say all families are different and what is good for one family may not be good for another family. I am not here to judge what you choose to do. However, I am here to tell you that whatever you choose, be ready to live with it as part of your choice.

One of the best ways to get young children to sleep is my trusted three B's Technique, which stands for Bath, Brush, Book, and Sweet Dreams.

Leave the room while your child is still awake. Kiss, hug, and say goodnight. By allowing your children to sleep on their own, they gain a sense of ownership and confidence and realize that they can self soothe. The earlier you accomplish this task, the less trouble you will have in the future getting your little one to sleep on his or her own.

Allow soft music or a nightlight. Remain calm when your child calls for you. Reassure your child that you will come back and check on him or her during the night. Always put your infant on his or her back in the crib to sleep. Impose reasonable consequences if your child refuses to go to sleep. For example, a child who comes out of the bedtime will receive the calm down corner or your child might lose TV time for continuing to act out at bedtime. Here are some recommended bedtimes based on the age of children:

2-5 years old 7:00pm - 7:30pm
6-11 years old 7:30pm - 8:00pm
12-14 years old 8:00pm - 9:00pm
15-18 years old
• 10:00pm for Freshmen and Sophomores
• 11:00pm - 12:00pm for Juniors and Seniors based on amount of homework
As your children get older, you will want to allow them more freedom. However, freedom does not mean they don't have a curfew or you go to sleep and they are not home. Practice structured freedom, which means you still control their goings and comings.

HOW TO HANDLE *CHORES*

Giving children chores beginning at 18 months can help foster responsibility and a sense of involvement and self-worth. Chores should be handled as necessary contributions to the family. After all if the dishes were never washed what would ultimately happen? If the trash was never taken out what would the house smell like? When you pose questions like these to children, they begin to understand the necessity of completing their chores.

Start early by having young children do simple chores like helping to bring clothes upstairs for you to fold. Remember that you are always in training mode. If we do not teach our children how to help in the household, they won't know how and eventually won't want to because they do not see the value in it. Three tips are below:

- Make doing chores a family affair
- Make it fun
- Praise and encourage children when they do their chore in excellence.

HOW TO HANDLE *THE ROLE OF DISCIPLINE*

You have heard me say it before. Discipline means to "teach." It is important to understand that your job as a parent is not to be your child's friend. You can have a close relationship with your child but don't get it twisted; you are not their friend. Their friends are found at the school and on the sports teams they engage in. When you are authoritative, loving, and lead in wisdom, children will respect you and value what you have to say. It is very difficult, if not impossible, to be their friend and discipline them at the same time. The role of a parent is to train and teach. You must never treat your child as your partner. Meaning, refrain from confiding in children because they are not emotionally mature enough to handle the adult conversation or emotional baggage that they might be left holding. In addition, refrain from drinking alcohol or partying with your child no matter how young you think you look or actually are. In essence, be a responsible parent that children can count on. When dealing with discipline, it is crucial that children know the rules. Once they know what the rules are, there needs to be consequences in place so that they know what is to be expected when they break a rule.

Make a commitment to say what you are going to do and do what you say if the rules are not followed. Don't make idle threats, as the children won't take you seriously, and you become less credible as a parent.

Make sure the punishment meets the crime. If your child talks back, for example, you may want to have them write 100 times that they will learn to tame their tongues by not talking back. For younger children, they may have to get something they like taken away from them. Popping a child in the mouth for being a smart mouth was a method my mother used. However, I wanted my child to realize that the first thing I would go to was not my hand or fist. It was still effective because as he got older he did not want to write or have his "electronic devices" taken from him, therefore he learned very early on that there are choices and consequences in life and it was up to him to be responsible enough to make the "right" choice

HOW TO HANDLE *PICKY EATERS*

Mealtimes must be vital in your home. That should be the one time when everyone gets together, sits down and eats. At the dinner table is when you will find out about your child's day. The dinner table is a time for good conversation and connecting with each other. Take every opportunity you can to eat at the same time. Make it a ritual in your home.

When your children are very young you are solely responsible for what they put in their stomachs. As they get older, and they develop more of a personality, they may start becoming picky eaters. When they are old enough to tell you they don't like something don't give them a free pass, and definitely don't make the mistake of cooking separate meals for them. No child has ever starved themselves. Your job as a parent is to put the food in front of them and encourage them to eat. The earlier you begin this process, the better. Follow these guidelines:

- If a child is not hungry, don't force it on him by bribing.
- Serve small portions to avoid waste.
- If your child does not eat at dinner time, make it clear that there will not be another meal made for him or her. (However, they still have to sit at the table with everyone)
- Don't offer dessert as a reward because children need to understand at an early age that they won't be rewarded for eating or punished for not eating.
- Minimize distractions at the dinner table: meaning no TV, cell phones or answering the phone when it is time for dinner.

Some of my trusted techniques are below:

Involvement Technique: Have your child help you go shopping to pick out the items for lunch and dinner, and then have them go the extra step and help you prepare the meal. Having the child help you by washing the vegetables or setting the table, or when older measuring out the items, will provide them with a sense of ownership.

Children are more likely to try to eat something that they helped to prepare.

Five Bites: It is important that children don't just say what they don't like without trying it. Parents should always encourage their children to take a minimum of five bites of various items on their plate. For example, if you are having baked chicken, mashed potatoes and spinach for dinner, the child under this technique has to taste the chicken, mashed potato and spinach at least once and then two more bites out of the three items on their plate. The theory is that when they "try" it, in most cases they will like it.

Don't give attention to the non eaters at the table: If you have two children and one child is not eating and the other one is, make sure you look at the one who is eating and say, "Oh my, I love the way _____(child's name) is trying all of their food and eating it." Children love to get attention and when the attention can be given in a positive way, the child will lean more toward it. If, for example, your focus was on the child who was not eating, you would be spinning your wheels all night by saying, "Why aren't you eating? You need to eat, you won't grow up to be strong if you don't eat." It doesn't work and prolongs the process.

Recipe Box: Children love to create with their parents. You can get a shoebox and label it with the child's name. Cut a hole in the top of the box and start putting your child's own recipes in it. Again, children feel special, it is fun, and they have a great time picking out and making what is on the recipe card.

HOW TO HANDLE **FAILURE**

I wanted to explain a little about failing. It is not necessary that your child always succeeds at a young age. For example, when my son was between five and eight years old, he and my husband would play basketball. Although my husband clearly had the advantage, he used to allow my son to win by falling and missing shots intentionally. I understood the spirit of it at the time. However, it did not help my son deal with the real world when he really did lose for the first time on the basketball court at seven-years-old. He completely broke down and cried because he had never been taught that "losing" and failing was a part of life. We, his parents, did him an injustice. From playing musical chairs, to cards, to sports allow your child at a young age to experience failure. They will be better equipped for it in the long run. Most of my valuable life lessons have stemmed from failing at something. That is the only way to improve and move forward.

Feast on This Thought
It doesn't matter how many times you fall down, it matters that you get back up.

HOW TO HANDLE **GRIEF**

Grieving is the natural process that helps us deal with tragedy and painful experiences in our lives. But children are not equipped with the coping skills to overcome a sudden shocking tragedy that leaves a void in their lives. We live in a world where guns are overtaking our communities and where children are killed every day. To help your child deal with a loss of their friend or loved one, here are some steps that you can use that will be helpful during this time:

- Don't tell the child you understand what they are going through because you really do not. Every child is different and will deal with grief in various ways.
- Listen to your children and take the time to answer their questions. When parents listen to their children's thoughts about death, they can help them to comprehend it better.
- Talk to your child honestly about the tragedy if they are asking you questions.
- Accept and help your children express their feelings about death. Whether your children are dealing with grief over the death of a grandparent or a pet, take their feelings of sadness seriously. I have had some younger children draw pictures about how they were feeling because they could not verbalize their feelings.
- Try to stick to the same routine so that things are not totally out of balance and confusing for the child. It provides for a sense of safety and security.
- Involve your children in the entire family's grieving process. Keep them with you as opposed to taking them to a baby sitter or a friend's house, particularly if they are over five years of age so that they are not alone in their feelings of sadness and loss.
- Most importantly, show affection by giving your child plenty of hugs and kisses.
- Explain to your child that death is a part of life that must be dealt with from everyone.
- Read books about losing a loved one.

• And finally, if the child is a preteen or older and feels the need to write a letter to the deceased because they did not get the opportunity to say something before they passed, allow them that time and space to do so.

HOW TO HANDLE *HOMEWORK*

Remember the vision you wrote for your child in the first chapter? Well hopefully within that vision you wrote that you wanted your child to have a good work ethic, manage responsibility, and work hard. Homework is an opportunity for children to gain time management skills, a strong work ethic, and the ability to prioritize. Stop getting angry with the child's teacher for assigning homework that you feel takes too long to do. Our job as parents is not to complain, but to encourage, motivate, and praise your child while they are doing their homework.

As noted earlier, you are your child's first teacher so it is imperative that you have the attitude of gratitude and that you show your child through words and actions that you think homework is important. Therefore:

• Set a regular time for homework.
• Provide a distraction-free workplace.
• Provide supplies so that children are not getting up every five minutes to sharpen their pencils, and identify what they are going to need to complete homework assignments.
• Set a good example with your tone and attitude. Make homework time a family affair so that the child doesn't feel like they are in it alone.

- Make doing homework fun not a chore. Rewards are a great incentive when children are young. As they get older, they need to gain a sense of "I am doing homework for me to gain knowledge and get better."
- Help but don't hover.
- Assist your child if they need it. But don't do the homework for them. That sends a poor message to your child that you don't have confidence in them to complete their own homework.
- Make sure you work with and know your child's teacher so that you never get to the end of a quarter or semester and have no idea that your child was failing or did not turn in homework.
- Be available for your child and look over completed assignments. I know it may take away from you watching television or checking emails or talking on the phone, but do it anyway. Remember it is not about you anymore. It is about your child getting what they need from you, and that is your time and attention.

HOW TO HANDLE *MESSY ROOMS*

I used to tell my child "Messy Room, Messy Life" meaning, when you have not learned how to clean your room effectively you will not clean your locker at school and eventually your office at work.

- Teach children early how to clean.
- Teach children what clean looks like. They must be able to visualize it before they are able to do it.
- Provide them with steps to make it easier.

- Make cleaning a family affair. Have Clean up Saturdays where they all pitch in and assist.

Most kids don't want to clean their rooms because they don't see the value in it. "Why do I need to make up my bed?" they say, "I am only going to get back into it tonight." As true as that may be, the truth of the matter is that they live in your house so you may require to have every room in the house look presentable and to your liking. I have found over the years that murmuring and complaining about why their room is not cleaned goes in one ear and out of the other. The best way to tackle the messy room is to tell your child, "Messy room, equals messy life. Start now to organize so that when you are older, you do not have to waste time learning how to clean a room, your office, your home, or your life."

Provide them with organizational steps of how to clean up their room.

Technique: Steps to a Tidy Room

1. Pick up all trash and place it in the garbage can.
2. Pick up all toys and put them in the box labeled 'toys.'
3. Hang up all of your clothes in the closet.
4. Put all dirty clothes in the hamper.
5. Place all books on the shelf.
6. Make up your bed.
7. Is everything done in excellence? If not, go back and make it excellent.

HOW TO HANDLE *DISRESPECT*

There is no way to handle disrespect from a child except to have zero tolerance for it. As soon as you hear the unkind words spoken to you, which could be as early as your child begins to talk, get very close to their face, look him or her right in their eyes, keep a stern look and voice and say, "I don't think so. It is not ok to speak unkindly to mommy or daddy. When mommy or daddy asks you to do something, you do it." Gently take their hand and show them what you asked them to do in the first place. It is called the "Tell and Show" technique.

Children who hit, slam doors, argue or raise their voices to parents are disrespectful. The Bible tells children to honor their mother and father. It does not come with a condition, meaning, it does not say honor your parent if they respect you or not. However, it does come with a consequence which is: so that thy days may be long. *(Exodus 20:12)* Trust that as children get older, around the preteen ages, they will begin to try your patience a lot more than the early years. The reason for that is mostly hormonal. However, if they are allowed to get away with it, they become more and more difficult to control. Parents must set boundaries very early. If a child is not corrected at two years-old they will be doing the same thing at four years-old. If it is not cute at two, be certain that it won't be cute at ten years-old. Follow these simple guidelines to maintain order in the house:

- Set boundaries early so children understand you have zero tolerance for disrespect.
- Set up house rules early to let children know

what is expected and not expected.
- Provide children with consistent consequences when they break a rule.
- Follow through with the consequences.
- Praise children when they are acting appropriately.

HOW TO HANDLE *SWEARING*

There are 225,000 words in the standard English dictionary with new words being added each day. Children can learn to use words other than those that are demeaning and disgusting. When children use profanity, it is most likely because they have heard it from someone else, prayerfully, not from you. I say it over and over again. It matters more what you do than what you say. It will be a lot easier for you to discipline (teach) your child about not using bad words if you aren't using them yourself.

Discuss "good" words and "bad" words with your child, letting them know that you expect them to only say good words in and outside of the home, whether you hear them or don't hear them. Your expectations of your children must be so strong in them that it does not matter whether you hear or see them. They will carry your expectations of them wherever they go in their spirit.

My mother used to say that only ignorant people use profanity, and that they are not intelligent enough to find and choose appropriate words so they take the easier road and say anything to get their point across. She also said people who use profanity have never learned how to control their temper. I don't know about you but I never wanted those two labels associated with me. Therefore, it was easy for me not to use those words and it increased my vocabulary.

If your child is old enough to write and has been taught not to use profanity and does so anyway, you may want to have him or her look up words in the dictionary that would replace the word they used and write a definition fifty to one hundred times. Always make the punishment "fit" the crime. That would be a good deterrent.

HOW TO HANDLE **NEGATIVITY**

Have you ever met a person that sees the glass half empty rather than half full? People who never see the bright side or a light at the end of the tunnel can be very draining. That behavior does not rear its ugly head only in adults. Children can be quite negative and pessimistic. That negativity usually begins in middle school but it is easy for parents to overlook the signs if it appears earlier. If your child begins to show signs of negativity, open the door of communication. Negative thinking isn't something that just plagues adults it also plagues children. There are some children who think negatively about themselves and their ability to accomplish anything.

I worked with a family who had three children. The middle child was extremely pessimistic. Nothing was ever right. He often claimed that he was not good in math or that his teacher and other students did not like him. He consistently became angry with himself and failed to try "new" activities unless he was sure that he could excel. He shut down in the face of obstacles claiming that "it was too hard." One of the techniques I found to be very helpful was my "Positivity Rulz" technique. The twelve year-old child and I made a replica of his head with a slit in the top. Each night before he went to bed, he had to write one positive comment about himself and every morning when he woke up before his feet hit the floor, he had to write another positive comment about himself. Over a span of a few weeks, his thoughts really began to change. When his thoughts began to change his actions followed. You can help your child by not giving into the "victim" mentality by flipping the script each time your child says something negative about themselves—contrast it by saying something positive.

HOW TO HANDLE *SELF-ESTEEM ISSUES*

A healthy self-esteem is like a child's armor against the challenges of the world. Children who know their strengths and weaknesses and feel good about themselves seem to have an easier time handling conflicts and resisting negative pressures. They tend to smile more readily and enjoy life. These kids are realistic and generally optimistic.

Parents can help their children develop a positive self-image in a number of ways:

- Get involved in your child's world by gaining wisdom and understanding. You may have to listen to what they are listening to on their ipod in order to understand where they are coming from and then have a discussion about it.
- Write "Love posts" into the heart, mind, and

spirit of your child. Meaning, speak those things that are not as though they were. For example, your child may not be applying himself or herself as well as he or she could be. Your "love post" at the end of that day could say, "I see Greatness in you and I know that you are capable of achieving your goals when you put your mind to it." That way children are left with something to reach for and aspire to, knowing that you believe in them.

- Encourage and praise your kids for a job well done.
- Focus on the positive.
- Value your child's voice.
- Validate your child by letting them know:
  ○ They are important
  ○ They are good enough
  ○ They mean the world to you.

(See Tools to build self-esteem at the end of the book)

HOW TO HANDLE *OTHER PEOPLE DISCIPLINING YOUR CHILD*

I don't know one successful child who has been raised in isolation. They had some teacher, some coach, some neighbor who planted seeds of success in that child that made him or her want to reach their Divine destiny.

- Embrace the help of others.
- Get your pride and ego out of the way...it is not about you.
- It takes a village and then some.

If your child is at my home and misbehaves it is not only my right but my duty to correct him or her. What if we all took the "it takes a village" mentality? I didn't birth your child but that doesn't mean that I don't care about his or her future. Just because you didn't birth a child doesn't mean that you cannot love a child.

I remember growing up, if we acted inappropriately at the corner store and a neighbor saw, they would correct us, and then before we made it home my mother was on the porch saying, "Mrs. so-and-so called and told me what happened at the store." You had to hear it all over again and you had better not get an attitude because the neighbor told. God says, I chasten you because I love you. So I believe wholeheartedly in correcting other people's children.

When your child is better, when our children are better, the world is a better place to live in. It is our responsibility to be our brother's and sister's keepers.

HOW TO HANDLE *STRESS DURING BUSY SEASONS*

During the holiday season, most of us spend our energy focusing on things like taking care of last minute details, thinking of ways that we can possibly purchase all of the gifts on our child's "Santa" list or planning and preparing for guests.

We attempt to say "yes" and cram into our already packed schedules every invitation to concerts, parties and dinners. We bribe our children into believing that Santa won't visit them if they have one more meltdown and by the end of the day we are completely stressed out and exhausted. As we hustle around, we often forget how difficult the holiday season can be for our children to adjust to. Here are some helpful hints to get you and your children through the holidays with ease.

Talk together – Turn off the technology and tune into the children. Sharing time, space and feelings is important during the holiday season. How well do I know my family?…is a game the entire family can play where each person guesses favorite colors, favorite foods, sport, television show, movie, artists etc. and the winner gets to skip chores like washing dishes.

Work together – involve children by keeping them busy and allowing them to help plan and prepare for the holiday season. When children take part in the decision-making, decorations and food prep, they gain a sense of empowerment and a sense of confidence that helps them stay accountable even toward their behavior.

Play together – board games are a wonderful way to get the entire family involved. Make arts and crafts together

Give together – Remember the reason for the season. This is a great time to start the family "food drive" and donate items to a local shelter.

- Make sure you are not entertaining the whims of children with long list of Christmas gifts. Manage their limitations by allowing them to list their 3-5 favorite gifts.
- Plan ahead what stores you are going to and what you will be purchasing. Also, make sure children are not tired or hungry when you go shopping.

- Involve your children by allowing them to do simple tasks. Finally, encourage an attitude of gratitude by doing something for someone else.

HOW TO HANDLE *MOM DOING ALL OF THE WORK*

This is going to sound really simple but if Mom is doing all the work and feeling like a maid I have one piece of advice for her. Stop doing it. You can't continue to do the same thing over and over and expect a different result.

Delegate to Others

We as women in particular have a hard time asking for help. We have that "I'm Every Woman" attitude and we have to realize that we cannot do everything 100% effectively without a little help from our friends and families. Let children know that everyone lives in the house and it is going to take each one of them to help keep the house clean.

HOW TO HANDLE *CHILDREN ON ELECTRONICS*

Technology is fine as long as it is not being abused by children. In the homes I visit, technology has become a major distraction. When children are allowed to be on their electronics, they are not spending time with the family bonding and strengthening relationships. I know it is "easier" to give your child a device like an ipad to keep them quiet but easy doesn't mean the best practice.

Secondly, technology also keeps children from MOVING. More than thirty percent of our nation's children are overweight. I need them to stop working those fingers texting and start working their bodies by exercising.

Create opportunities to be outdoors, playing, running and jumping with children. That way they increase their gross motor, communication, team building and social skills. The benefits are so much greater than sitting around on the computer or in front of the television.

Therefore, try limiting the amount of "tech" time. There should be no use of electronics during the week with the exception of needing it for a research project for school. Try a one-hour per day limit during the weekends. Take note that children do not miss what they don't have. The evening schedule should be as follows: Do homework, prepare for dinner, spend some family time together and get ready for bed. When you allow children to play on electronics two to four hours before going to bed, it is difficult for them to wind down and obtain a peaceful rest.

HOW TO HANDLE THE CHILDREN *WHEN A NEW SIBLING ARRIVES*

Another challenge that you will have to overcome is how to react to your other children when a new baby arrives. I have some help for you. Congratulations! The best advice I can give parents who are welcoming another addition into the family is to be patient. Understand that it is a perfectly natural tendency of many children to feel resentful of their new younger brother or sister. I don't think you can prevent feelings of jealousy or envy but you can be proactive and prepare them in advance.

For example, involve the child in the process. Even before the baby arrives. Talk about where the baby is in Mommy's tummy or if you are adopting, where the baby is coming from. Encourage the child to give the baby hugs and kisses goodnight. When reading a bedtime story, have the child present so that the baby can hear the voice of the child as well. The more the older child feels like you are including him or her in the process the smoother the transition will be. Even when the baby arrives, explain to the child that the baby will need more attention since it is younger. When changing a diaper have the older child take the diaper out of the diaper bag and give you the diaper cream. Small helping hands can go a long way in making the child feel like they matter too. The more you are able to make the first child feel like they are involved in the entire process, the less you have to worry about the older child acting out to gain attention.

Key Points:

- Teach soft and gentle touches.
- Demonstrate how to talk to and take care of the baby (model the behavior you want the child to pick up on).
- Praise the child for doing a great job as an older sibling.
- Make "special time" with older child.

HOW TO HANDLE *A SEPARATION OR DIVORCE*

Adversity in life can be difficult and even more challenging for a child. For children, divorce and separation of parents can be stressful, sad and confusing. My mother and father separated when I was twelve years old. The hole in the soul that a child feels when a parent leaves is sometimes unbearable. As a parent, you can make the process and its effects less painful for your children. Helping your children cope with divorce means providing stability in your home and attending to your children's needs with a reassuring, positive attitude.

As a parent, it is normal to feel uncertain about how to give your children the right support through your divorce or separation. It is important to keep a few things in mind:

• Keep the lines of communication open—Your child may deal with his or her emotions by shutting down and getting angry. That is your opportunity as the parent to talk to your child about what he or she is feeling.

• Be patient—Most children do not bounce back overnight and some transitions may take longer than others. Do not rush your child's time clock. Have the patience to allow them to go through their "process."

• Be understanding of what your child is going through. Don't pass it off as being unimportant. Children have a way of picking up on our inability to seem interested when we are perfectly uninterested.

• Provide as much age appropriate advance notice and/or explanation as possible so that the child seemingly understands what is going to happen. Do not keep children in the dark.

• Be observant and take anecdotes of long lasting changes in behavior, eating, and lack of communication.

If the changes in behavior persists and you see your child withdrawing, you may have to seek professional help, such as a licensed social worker or child psychologist.

HOW TO HANDLE *EATING AT A RESTAURANT*

I am not the only one that gets crazy when I am at a beautiful restaurant and there are children screaming, hollering, touching everything (including others), running around right in front of their permissive parents.

Food for Thought: Remember that mealtime manners should begin at *home* rather than the restaurant.

When you are eating out, there are a few things you can do to prevent restaurant mealtime mayhem.

- Give children advance notice that the family will be eating at a restaurant. This is important so that they can prepare themselves.
- Provide visual restaurant rules:
  ○ Leave condiments alone.
  ○ Sit at the table.
  ○ Use your manners.
  ○ Use listening ears.
- Bring drawing materials for your children in case they get bored.
- Praise your children for good behavior.

Oftentimes, parents forget to do the praising and encouraging part. We are so focused on criticizing and correcting their negative behavior that we forget to see them when they are acting in appropriate ways. It is just as important to not only correct but also to compliment.

HOW TO HANDLE **SIBLING RIVALRY**

When I see siblings not getting along to the extent that they constantly fight it is usually because they have not been taught "HOW TO" play together. They are vying for attention. Children don't care whether it is negative attention or positive attention as long as they get it. If you are having issues with children being at each other's throats do the following:

Create activities that are designed to bring them together. Group the 5 and 7-year-old together, and the 9 and 12-year-old together. Then it is time to start strengthening their relationship with each other.

Fun games that bring children together are:

- Relay races
- Potato sack – reward them when they are helping each other out, encouraging each other, taking turns.
- Scavenger hunts – one child is blindfolded and the other has to lead and guide them and eventually learn to trust them.
- Use Kindness cards – children go around the circle and choose a card, then on the card they have to say something nice about the person sitting next to them, creating a habit.
- How well do I know my sister/brother?
- Favorite color?
- Favorite team?
- My sister is great at _____?

HOW TO HANDLE **CHILDREN MAKING EXCUSES**

The major problem with making excuses and giving explanations is that it doesn't help the child learn to manage himself or herself or to perform. Your child has to learn how to solve problems and make good choices.

Children shouldn't be allowed to blame other people, places or things for not meeting expectations or completing tasks. Parents need to model the behavior they want. Parents should be accountable and take ownership when they make mistakes. Just because you are a parent does not mean you cannot apologize. When my child used to make excuses for his lack of doing something, I would make him recite the following quote by an unknown author and then write it ten times.

Excuses are tools of the incompetent
which create monuments of nothingness.
Those who specialize in them
are seldom good in anything...

~Anonymous

HOW TO HANDLE **TEMPER TANTRUMS**

Temper Tantrums are extremely common in toddlers and preschoolers. Tantrums are how young children deal with difficult feelings.

One of the first things to recognize is that it helps to avoid situations that may trigger tantrums. For example, if your child is tired, hungry, or over stimulated, they are more likely to have tantrums.

Parents should not give in to children to avoid a tantrum. The reason being is that it sets a bad precedent and children begin to realize that having a tantrum gets me what I want. Even though "giving in" to your child is detrimental to them I see parents doing this all the time. The fact that they just want peace and quiet is the reason why they say they give in. However, what parents are not realizing is that the supposed peace and quiet for the moment leads to chaos and confusion later because they are failing to teach their child how to handle their feelings appropriately.

It is important to teach children self-control and that there are consequences to the tantrum. One major consequence is that they will not get what they are having the tantrum over. So if a child wants a toy and is having a tantrum over the toy, the best consequence is to not give the child the toy.

Steps to Handling Temper Tantrums

Temper tantrums are something every child has…and many of…it's also not uncommon to have them at different ages and through adolescence. We should stop teaching our children never to be angry, but rather teach them how to be angry and how to behave and communicate effectively.

Although temper tantrums are extremely common in toddlers and preschoolers, that doesn't make a parent feel more comfortable or less embarrassed when temper tantrums occur. Below are some helpful things to do before and after the tantrum ensues.

Tips for 2-year-old tantrums

1. Create Positive House Rules children will expect and understand. They should be written in a positive way avoiding the words no and don't placed at the child's level and have visual cues so that younger children can recognize and understand them.
2. Put Immediate Consequences in Place to clearly define what's acceptable.
3. Don't Give into the Tantrum and reward your child's bad behavior by giving in because this is the behavior that will be learned.
4. Remain Calm so the tantrum is not escalated by your reaction.

Tips for 5-year-old tantrums

1. Respond Don't React! Don't give them the negative attention they want and don't fight anger with anger.
2. Cling to Consistency—Don't Negotiate—basically follow the same warning and consequence procedure each time so the child knows what to expect.
3. Correct Negative Behavior with Consequences. This can be a "lose what you like" or "calm down corner" depending on the child.
4. Eliminate Guilt—feeling bad is an excuse. Your job as a parent is to teach and train. If you love your child you will correct them.

Tips for teenage tantrums

1. Set Boundaries & Implement punishment for your tween or teen.
2. Talk Openly without Judgment. An angry teenager

who's allowed to express himself or herself will feel less pressure and build up less anxiety.

3. Gain Wisdom & Understanding of what is going on in their world. Pay close attention to the changes in their lives.

4. Show Respect with Your Actions. It's important to deal with a teenager by showing them respect as the individual they are trying to become.

5. Don't allow children to disrespect you without an immediate consequence.

HOW TO HANDLE *CO-PARENTING*

It took two parents to make the child, so let's not drop the ball on parenting in the hands of only one parent. As I travel across this country I have noticed that one parent seems to be more involved with the children than the other. There was one home I went to where the father looked like he was a "stranger" in his own home. He did not take the time to really listen or understand his children. Instead he escaped to the garage or the office away from the children. This kind of behavior puts a barrier between the children and the absent parent (as I call them) and also creates a problem for the relationship between the parents.

Here are some basic tips for co-parenting:

- Cooperate with each other as much as possible. For example, help each other out with chores or duties, such as bathing the children or reading stories before bedtime.
- Participate in family time as much as possible.

For example, play a family game together on the weekend. And during the week each parent should make time to spend at least 15 minutes with each child just being together.

• Keep each other informed of what's going on when it comes to the child's schooling and medical appointments, so that both parents are well abreast. In one of the families I work with the parents had split shifts so when the father came home from work the mother went right out the door to go to work. It was as if they were two ships passing in the night. I gave them a technique of using a communication board to write notes to each other so that everyone would be informed as to what went on throughout the entire day.

I am often asked what my Top Parenting Rules are that are necessary for all parents in order to meet the challenges of parenting:

TOP FIVE PARENTING RULES TO MEET THE CHALLENGE

- Do set limits and guidelines for your children. By setting guidelines children know what is expected. This can be accomplished by creating clear, simple, and positive house rules, such as gentle touches, use inside voices, or be kind to each other.
- Do praise and encourage your children. Children should always be praised and encouraged for doing the "right" thing. Children are attention seekers. When the attention is given to them for doing something positive, parents will begin to see more of the positive behavior.
- Do follow through and be consistent. So many parents fail to follow through with discipline. If a child breaks a rule, they must be consistently corrected. That is the only way that they will learn that poor choices have negative consequences. Parents will not be teaching a lesson for the moment, they will be teaching a lesson for life.
- Do not lie to your children. Model the behavior you want. You should not tell your children not to lie but then you lie. It sets a poor example for children.
- Do understand that no family is perfect but you are required to do your best. You can never give up as long as you have breath in your body. There is always hope for your children, hope for your family, and hope for America.

CHAPTER FOUR

DESSERT

*Our children deserve the Fruit of the Spirit
when raising them.*

After eating the entre, the server will usually ask you if
you want dessert. In my opinion, dessert is the best part
of the meal and as such it is also the best part of parenting.
Why do I say that? In most cases, dessert is full of calories
and saturated fats and may not be as healthy for you
unless you choose the healthier choice like FRUIT.

As a parent, it is important that just as we began with
the appetizer, which was ourselves, we end with ourselves
providing our children with the fruit of the spirit. I would
be lying if I told you that it was easy to choose fruit over
a large slice of red velvet cake. It is not. However, in the
end, your children will appreciate the lessons learned
from your choice, just as our bodies will appreciate the
healthier choice. So let's get to it.

Longsuffering (Romans 5:3)

You will not get through life without problems, pains, challenges, and suffering, especially during the parenting journey. Your child's process is going to be different from another child's process. It is uniquely designed for them to make and mold them into what God would have for them to be. It is necessary for you to be prayed up at all times. Don't wait until there is a problem before you decide to ask God for help in raising your child. We rarely have the answers and what used to work for your parents and grandparents no longer works for this generation of children.

Today's children have access to more knowledge yet have less wisdom. Wisdom and understanding come by way of experiences. Since we live in a microwave society where everyone wants the "quick fix," it is difficult to get the lesson because no one wants to take the time to go through the process and do the work to get to a place where we are learning from our mistakes. When your children make poor choices, and they will, take the time to communicate with them through their decision making process. Ask the question, "What could you have done differently that would have resulted in a better outcome?" That is how children grow and develop and learn in the process.

Longsuffering means that you might not have the answer or even see the answer ahead. But through it all, know that all things work together, *(Romans 8:28)* and even if you never understand why your child's life journey went down a road that you would have liked to see less traveled, as long as you have the faith and strength to make it through it with them, victory is on the other side of the mountain.

Many of us face hardships in parenting, but we must never give up on God! Although the valleys seem dark and it does appear that "we are troubled on every side, distressed, persecuted and cast down," but in the eyes of our faithful God, "we are not distressed, not in despair, not forsaken and not destroyed." *(2 Corinthians 4:8-9)*

We are loved by God and He desires that we live the abundant life. His abundant life only comes from dying to self and living for Christ. He is a God that loves to have His children bear fruit. It's *not* the same fruit that the world bears. It is the wealth that never rusts and never passes away—the fruit of the spirit. Through the many trials of my life, I know that all is Father-filtered. He is pruning me and I am beginning to bring forth that precious fruit. The fruit of longsuffering has been the most painful to birth and I have resisted the process many days. But, through it all, I have learned to trust God.

GENTLENESS *(1 Peter 3:15)*

"I choose gentleness...nothing is won by force. I choose to be gentle. If I raise my voice may it be only in praise. If I clench my fist, may it be only in prayer. If I make a demand, may it be only of myself."

~**Max Lucado**

When you think of how we handle infants words like

'gentle' come to mind. However, as children get older and older our gentleness dissipates. Don't confuse gentleness with spoiling. We can be gentle in our responses to our children instead of being harsh and unreasonable to them. We can answer their questions in a gentle way even if we think to ourselves, how in the world could they have asked that question? Gentleness is more about being considerate, amiable, kind and tender, not harsh and scornful. It is not hard to understand why we are not gentle with our children. We are often overly stressed, overworked, out of balance and overloaded with so much work that we barely have time for ourselves, much less our children. However, that can never be the excuse for treating our children in a way that is not gentle.

The Bible says "A gentle tongue is a tree of life; But perverseness therein is a breaking of the spirit." *(Proverbs 15:4)*

GOODNESS *(Psalms 23:6)*

Surely goodness and mercy shall follow me all the days of my life: and I will dwell in the house of the LORD for ever.

Goodness is the state or quality of being good, virtuous or morally excellent. This is one of the most important character traits we can possess. Goodness should begin in our speech. Parents need to speak well of their spouse or the child's father. Remember that children identify themselves as being part of both parents. Some mothers make the mistake of emasculating the father by speaking down to him in front of the children or talking to the child about things that are for adult ears only. When parents make that mistake, children have less respect for their fathers simply because the mother has taught the child that it is okay to do so by their own words. The same is true for the father who does not speak kindly of the mother. Never speak unkindly of one another. Don't be double-minded by saying one thing and doing another. Refrain from gossiping or back stabbing each other. Be a man and woman of honor and excellence so that your children can look to you as a great example that has provided them with a solid foundation for future success.

Love (I John 4:16)

And we have come to know and have believed the love which God has for us. God is love, and the one who abides in love abides in God, and God abides in him.

How do you really define love? Love has never been about material things that you give your child because you want them to have a better childhood than you did. You have heard me say it over and over. Love to a child means TIME.

Time is taking intimate moments each day to spend talking, sharing, playing together, not just being in the child's presence. Have you ever been in the same room with someone and not spent time with them? It is just like being alone. Children need to have your undivided attention, so when you are home with them be home. Stay off the phone gossiping, don't work on your computer until they go to bed. Again, spending time with them doesn't mean transporting them to and from soccer practice or some other sporting, extracurricular activity. They know the difference. They want a piece of your heart, mind and soul, and that takes precious time to give. I have been fortunate enough to have had my son with me for the first five years of his life at my schools. However, when he went to elementary school, I made a point of us having a special day together where just he and I would spend part of the day talking, golfing, going to lunch, or just walking. I wanted to take the opportunity to sow into his life and those times were so special. They never stopped. When he went to college we chose a day where it could be just the two of us. I am constantly amazed that he not only liked our meetings, he looked forward to them. The special time was a chance to get to know how he thought and the kind of decision making processes he had. It helped me to know him better and for him to get to know me. At each stage of your child's life they are changing, growing, and developing. If you are privileged enough to go along for the ride, it can be a gratifying experience.

Joy (James 1:2-4)

Joy is something that each parent must aspire to. It is unlike happiness in that feelings of happiness change depending on your mood. Joy is something that comes from deep within. That never leaves you whether you are having a good day or a difficult day, whether it is sunny outside or raining, whether you are going through a trial or just coming out of one. Joy is something that your children must see in you. We talked about setting a standard and having someone to measure up to. Your child, no matter what situation you find yourself in, will always look to you, their earthy mother and father, until they are spiritually mature enough to rely on their Heavenly Father that will never leave or forsake them. Joy is something that your child must know is a constant in your life. The world didn't give it to them, so the world can't take it away. The joy of the Lord is truly your strength.

PEACE *(John 14:27)*

You will have many opportunities as parents to provide peace in your home. Make your home a safe haven for children. A place for them to come for security knowing that even when they make bad decisions and have to suffer the consequences of their actions, there will be a peaceful place to go: a place of comfort where no hurt, harm or danger can come to them. As a father one of your jobs is that of a provider and a protector and children are looking to you to be a leader of the household. If the mother is the sole provider then you have to be the provider and protector of your children. In the early 1990's the family dynamics of the household began to change drastically. Both parents were forced to work because it was very difficult to live off of one income. With both parents out of the house and working long hours, children were left to their own devices by becoming "latch key" kids. Gone were the days of Mom or Dad being home when you arrived from school for an afternoon snack, homework, and helping to prepare dinner for the family. Now the routine was the child was left to let themselves in the house, make a snack, and more than likely chose to do other things that did not include homework. They are not to blame. On the one hand, it forced them to be more independent. However, it also gave them a false sense of authority. Children need to be taught. Children need to be trained. They are not meant to be thrown into situations that they are not readily able to handle. You and I, as parents, must make sure our children are protected, provided for, and have the peace of the household to make them feel like the words Dorothy uttered over and over again in the Wizard of Oz, "There is no place like home."

FAITH (Hebrews 11:1)

The Bible says in Hebrews 11:1, "Now faith is the substance of things hoped for and the evidence of things not seen."

If we don't do anything else as parents we must give our children the opportunity to experience what faith is. The problem is you cannot give what you don't have. So parents must have unshakable faith. We must have mountain moving faith and faith that withstands the test of time.

The journey of parenting is difficult and there will be times when you won't know what is going on with your child or the world. However, we have to hold fast to the promises of God and know that we don't know what tomorrow holds but we do know who holds tomorrow. God is our refuge in the time of trouble.

With God we live, we move and have our very being, so it is only natural to look to Him, the creator of all things. Faith is like a muscle; it needs to be exercised in order to become stronger. All I pray for now is strength and to be whatever God would have me to be. When our children see how strong our faith walk is despite the hell all around us, they are inspired to allow the Lord to use them as vessels for the Glory of God.

Temperance—Self-control (Romans 12:1)

"I appeal to you therefore, brothers, by the mercies of God, to present your bodies as a living sacrifice, holy and acceptable to God, which is your spiritual worship. Do not be conformed to this world, but be transformed by the renewal of your mind, that by testing you may discern what is the will of God, what is good and acceptable and perfect."

When you get angry very quickly and raise your hand or worse fist to children in anger you are out of control and out of the order of God. Stop talking to me about spare the rod if you are not willing to follow the complete Bible. God is love. Even when he disciplines us it is in love. Yes, we may even get slapped around by God after being disobedient time and time again. But even God gives us warnings and allows us to repent and turn from our wicked ways. The beatings that I see happening in America today are not what is outlined in the Bible. Children are not supposed to die from the hand of a parent or lack of control. Children are not to be humiliated and debased because you, the parent, are unable to control what you say and how you react. I often tell parents no one promised you a rose garden. There will be times when our children will make us so angry that we want to almost "kill" them, not literally. Although, my mom used to say, "I brought you into this world and I will take you out." However, we must maintain a controlled response and not react in harsh anger. Always have enough control over your emotions to take a moment and count to 5, 10 or 100 depending on how angry you are and then respond. Children are always watching us and the way you handle them and others will often determine the way they will grow up to handle their own problems and conflicts.

CHAPTER FIVE

· · · · · · · · · · · · ·

WHAT IS THE COST (OF THE MEAL)

Parenting Commitment will cost you to SACRIFICE

Oh yes, it is going to cost you something. As wonderful as it is to be a parent, we cannot get through this parenting journey successfully without sacrifice. The definition of sacrifice is a loss or something you give up, usually for the sake of a better cause. Parents sacrifice time and sleep to take care of their children. Sometimes parents sacrifice their dreams so that their children will obtain theirs. I would like to look at sacrifice in another vein. The word SACRIFICE is made up of SACRI and FICIO, which means TO MAKE HOLY. Rather than looking at sacrifice as negative, look at it as the means to our goal and a step toward excellence. The dedication and commitment that it takes to make the life of your child the best it can be will take sacrifice. Sacrifice at its essence is really about gain not loss.

You can do no greater job than to sacrifice your wants for their needs. It is one of the greatest gifts we can give to our children. Once you know what needs to be done to raise children in today's society, your sacrifice will be well worth the outcome of living to see them reach their full potential.

PARENTING COMMITMENT WILL COST YOU TO BE SELFLESS

I am so tired of seeing parents have child after child believing that they can still do and live the way they did before they had children. Why would anyone think that it is okay to have children only to leave them with other people so that you the parent can still hang out until all hours of the night partying with associates (EVERY WEEKEND) Really? You have to become selfless and know that it is NOT about you and never really should have been about you in the first place. Our children must become the priority after God and our spouses. This does not mean to neglect your health and your welfare. However, it does mean your priorities must be placed in order so that children receive the best of you at all times, not grandma, auntie or uncles. You are the parent and it is selfish of you to pawn your children off to others particularly if it is done more than occasionally.

Food for Thought:

> *Your mind's selfishness*
> *Is your all-exclusive individuality.*
> *Your heart's selflessness*
> *Is your all-inclusive universality.*
>
> ~**Sri Chinmoy**

PARENTING COMMITMENT WILL COST YOU TO SERVE

Martin Luther King said it best when he said anybody can be great because everybody can serve...you only need a heart full of grace and a soul generated by love. As we raise our children know that your service to them is really your service to God. When you raise children the best you can doing all that you know is right and true, you will be doing a great service to our creator, to the child and to the world. When each of us takes the time to raise compassionate, productive children the world is a brighter place because they are in it.

It won't be about your flesh and what YOU want; it will be about what works best for your child.

Dear God,

Thank you for all children. Protect them and help them to continue to grow in you. Give us wisdom to teach them to show them love and your way. Thank you for the way they are teaching us the adults and for the privilege to be a small but crucial part of their journey. Help us as parents to use our hands to hold them close, our ears to listen to them when we don't want to hear what they are saying, our eyes to see when they hurt, our nose to smell the sweet scent of their innocence, our mouth to speak words of wisdom, our legs to walk and run alongside them as they grow and develop.

God has a heart for children and we should as well

whether we birthed them or not. We are responsible for being a member of the "village" that binds children together; the thread that mends lives and the bridge that allows our children to walk into greatness. Can we do it? I believe we can.

One of the greatest messages is in the book of Mark which calls for us to serve others even as Jesus served. *(Mark 10:45)* Through His words and actions Jesus portrays Service and self-sacrifice as the hallmark of true greatness.

CHAPTER SIX

PARENTING TIPS

As I mentioned in the beginning, this book is designed to read like a menu and I never like to leave a good restaurant without providing gratuity or a (tip). As I travel around this country so many people have asked what my top parenting tips are for raising children in today's society? Many of these final parenting tips are throughout the book. However, it is important for me to reiterate the ones that have made an impact in the life of my child and hopefully in the lives of families and children across America.

MY TOP TEN PARENTING TIPS

1. Never Give up Hope

Hope is something that we as parents must continue to have for our children. All children have their own journey to travel. Sometimes, they will make good choices and sometimes they will make bad choices. When they make bad choices from two years old when they begin talking back to eighteen years old, you must provide them with consequences for their actions. When you do not allow children to get away with negative behavior, the behavior eventually ceases. You can never be too tired, overwhelmed or in despair that you give up hope. Your children are worth the effort. They are worth the time spent talking to them, reading to them, bonding with them, connecting with them. Love them enough to give them hope of a bright future.

2. Always speak positively of the child's mother and father.

You may or may not be married to your child's mother or father. Whatever the case, never speak unkind words about the child's parent. This can be one of the most detrimental things that you can do as a parent. Children understand at a very early age that they are a part of both mom and dad. Therefore, if mom is speaking unkindly about dad or vice versa, the child begins to have feelings of inadequacy, which will breed insecurity. Keep any negative comments about the other parents away from the ears of children and above all, always let the child know that both parents love them very much. Both parents need to remain active in their child's life. It is a travesty to allow your anger and resentment to keep another parent away from the child. Remember that it is not about "you." From the first day that your child is born, it really becomes about them and doing everything in your power that is in the best interest of the child.

3. Model the behavior you want

Too many parents are dishonest, unkind, swear and gossip to name a few and expect that their children will not do the same. Children are great observers. They are watching your every move and if you are not careful they will pick up your worse habits and parade them around for the entire world to see. If you want to give your child anything, start with giving them a secure, well-adjusted, confident, honest, loving, positive woman and man of integrity and character. Model those qualities so that they grow up emulating the greatness in you.

4. Speak Life into your child

When I talk about speaking life to children, I am saying make the words that come out of your mouth positive. It is time-out for being negative and speaking down to children. Your words are life changing and long lasting and it is up to you to make sure that you are speaking words of encouragement at all times. Even when the child is misbehaving, address the actual "behavior" instead of the child. For example, never say, "why are you so bad?" The behavior is what is "bad" not the total essence of the child. If you don't like the child's mother or father, that does not give you the right to speak ill of the child. Whatever you speak is what they will eventually become.

5. Spend real time getting to know your child

At each stage of your child's development, there will be opportunities for you to get to know them better. You hear me say it all the time. Love to a child is spelled T.I.M.E. The more quality time you spend with a child, the more they feel secure and loved. I say quality because some parents believe that driving their children to basketball or ballet class is quality time. What matters most to a child is that the time you spend with them is just for them. Being on your cell phone when you walk into the doors of the school, not listening to your child when they talk to you about their day because you are too distracted doing other things does not make children feel loved and wanted.

6. Be Consistent and Follow-through
I cannot tell you how important it is to be consistent with children. When you say that you are going to do something, please do it. When you are inconsistent, your child will not be able to trust you or your word. We as parents are instructed to train up children in the way they should go. When parents are inconsistent and do not follow through with their words and actions, children get confused and find it difficult to listen to instructions.

7. Set Guidelines and Boundaries
Children need to understand at a very early age that there are things that they will and will not be allowed to do as children. You, the parent are responsible for setting up those guidelines and boundaries so that children do not attempt to cross them. We are a society, which is governed by rules, and your family should be governed by rules as well. If we provide children with simple, common sense instructions on what they should and should not do and follow through every time with punitive consequences, the child will become trained to listen respectfully to you. They may not always like it, but they will be better for it.

8. Allow your child to Dream
Some parents are "dream killers." They don't mean to be but because they are so stuck in their own reality of what held them back or what they were not able to accomplish they force that same mindset on their children. You

may have never graduated from college. That does not mean your child cannot attend, graduate and become successful. You may not have ever been an entrepreneur but that doesn't mean your child can't think outside of the box and become anything he or she aspires to be. When you encourage children to operate in excellence and to reach for their dreams through hard work, dedication and commitment, they will be able to do it. Sometimes, just you believing in them will push them to a higher level of expectation.

9. Share your experiences with children

Children need to hear your stories about growing up that are developmentally age appropriate for them to hear. When we share our experiences, our children learn that they are not alone and that we as parents made and are still making mistakes. As we learn from our mistakes we will continue to grow and develop into the man and woman God would have for us to be.

10. Let Go and Allow God

In order for a caterpillar to transform into a beautiful butterfly it must go through a "process." The same is true for children. There will be times when you are so pleased with your children because they are listening, respectful, helpful and loving. Other times, you will be thinking "where did this child come from?" but through it all know that your children's lives are in the hands of God and only He can make, mold and design them into wonderfully, compassionate human beings. Our job as parents is to be positioned to adequately raise, educate, nurture and train our children. There will be those times when we have to take our hands off the steering wheel and allow God to order and direct every area of our lives including our children. In fact, it is our duty to take our hands off the steering wheel because God is a better driver.

The road to being a successful parent is not straight. There is a curve called Failures, a loop called Mistakes, speed bumps called Setbacks, red lights called Anger, caution lights called Frustration. You will have flats called Disobedience. But, if you have a spare called Commitment, an engine called Perseverance, insurance called Faith, and a driver called Jesus, you will make it to a place of successful parenting, realizing that your best was good enough.

THE END
(but as a parent, it never really ends...)

Parenting Tools

House Rules

Steps to a Tidy Room

Choices and Consequence cards

Self Reliance Chart

Kindness Cards

Self Reflection Book for Tweens and Teens

Love Posts

Deposits of Greatness

Positivity Rulz Cards

And much much more...

Tools Available to order online at www.deborahltillman.com/greaterparentingsystem/products.

ABOUT THE AUTHOR

• • • • • • • • • • • • •

Deborah L. Tillman M.S. Ed

America's Most Authentic and Powerful
Parent Educator

TRANSFORMING *PARENTS* IN AMERICA

Deborah L. Tillman is a Parent Educator, Speaker, Author, Founder and CEO of Happy Home Child Learning Center Inc., located in Northern Virginia and "America's Supernanny" on Lifetime Television.

Labeled "A Force for Good" by the Washington Post, Tillman has a deep passion for children. Her mission is to transform parents and encourage them to be the best they can be. She began her career over a decade ago when she became frustrated with the lack of quality childcare her son was receiving. So she quit her very lucrative accounting job and started her own school in 1994. Tillman believes that "schools and educators should not have to do for children what we as parents were designed to be doing." Tillman says, "It is not about making a child; it is about raising a child."

Deborah L. Tillman is America's most authentic and powerful voice for parents and is not afraid to be open and honest with them. Her no-nonsense yet, loving approach landed her the role as America's Supernanny on Lifetime Television. Tillman holds a Master's Degree in Early Childhood Special Education from George Washington University and is currently seeking her Doctorate.

Among her many acknowledgements, Deborah Tillman has been a recurring Parenting Expert on the Steve Harvey Talk show. She has also been seen on the View, Today Show, Katie Show, Home and Family Network, Wendy Williams and CNN to name a few. Tillman has also been featured in Essence Magazine, Jet, Ebony, Northern Virginia, Washington Woman and Parent Magazines. Tillman has contributed articles to Gospel Today magazine.

Tillman is the author of "Stepping out On Faith"- How to Open a Quality Childcare Center (2005) and "Parenting on Purpose" (2014), A Menu for Raising Children in Today's Society.

Tillman is a highly sought after facilitator and speaker. Her commitment, persistence, courage, tenacity and love for children and their families keep her going. It is Tillman's belief that it does not always take a "village" to raise children; it takes a Parent who is *P*ositioned to *A*dequately, *R*aise, *E*ducate, *N*urture and *T*rain the future generation.

Tillman contends that there can be only one winner on the basketball court...but we can all be winners in America when our children are raised with a solid foundation for future success.

Mrs. Tillman lives in Northern Virginia with her husband, James, and their son, Zeplyn, who is a graduate of Georgetown University.

To purchase any of Mrs. Tillman's Greater Parenting
System Tools, visit her website at:
www.deborahltillman.com
Twitter@deborahltillman